THE ZEAL OF THY HOUSE

THE ZEAL OF THY HOUSE

by

DOROTHY L. SAYERS

WIPF & STOCK · Eugene, Oregon

Wipf and Stock Publishers
199 W 8th Ave, Suite 3
Eugene, OR 97401

The Zeal of thy House
By Sayers, Dorothy L. and Irving, Laurence
Copyright©1937 by Sayers, Dorothy L.
ISBN 13: 978-1-61097-023-5
Publication date 8/1/2011
Previously published by Victor Gollancz Ltd, 1937

Dedicated to the Dorothy L. Sayers Society
that has generously sponsored
the production
of this 2011 series edition

For more information about the DLS Society
please turn to the last page of this book

Introduction to the 2011 Series Edition

On the occasion of the republication of some of Dorothy Leigh Sayers' plays, we pay tribute to a most remarkable person: a literary entrepreneur of no mean order, a lay theologian in an age when it was almost unthinkable for a woman to be acknowledged as a theologian, a thinker who pioneered new ways of engaging audiences with central Christian dogmas as rehearsed in the Church's creeds. The final flowering of her work was connected with her rediscovery of Dante's *Divine Comedy*, which stimulated her to produce some of her finest work, including the play she personally thought was her very best. She did not set out to be a writer of 'religious' drama, but her experience of life through a traumatic era of European history, together with her special talents, made such drama part of her legacy to us.

Born in 1893 at the tail-end of the Victorian era, Dorothy was the only child of well-educated parents. She was baptised in Christ Church, Oxford, (Diocesan Cathedral as well as College Chapel) where her father, an ordained clergyman of the Church of England, was Headmaster of the school which educated the boys who sang in the choir. In 1897 her father accepted a Christ Church living in the 'Fens' (drained, hedgeless farmland) about sixteen miles from Cambridge, and together with her mother, a series of governesses and a brief experience of school from age fifteen, she received an excellent education which suited her particular talents. She emerged into adulthood holding to a number of strong convictions, one of which was about the importance of vigorous and clear thinking and speaking about Christian dogma, enlivening the real and varied existences of human beings in all their complexity. Entry to Somerville College, Oxford in 1912 placed DLS among a very favoured few in the Britain of her day, though privilege sheltered no one from the miseries of World War 1 as some of her early published poetry reveals. In any event, her 'Hymn in Contemplation of Sudden Death' (1916)[1] transcends its origins in wartime, though was to come into its own especially in the appalling era of aerial bombing of civilians in the new horrors of World War 11. This is of central importance for the cathedral play written for Lichfield, as we shall see.

So far as World War I is concerned, DLS' detective fiction reflects something of the world of the survivors and the bereaved, and we note here that she never isolated herself from the social and political struggles of her day. Some of her sensitivities are displayed in the development of her portrait of her aristocratic sleuth, Peter Wimsey. He struggles with 'shell-shock' and the memory of having had to give orders which sent so many to their deaths, and as a sleuth he is responsible too for other deaths in a country which still enforced capital punishment. A priority for DLS of course was to find ways of earning her own living, whilst also negotiating a series of love-relationships amongst the somewhat problematic selection of available men of her social class and education post-1918. A man who was not 'marriageable' became the father of her son, her only child, and she simply had to earn money to support Anthony, brought up as he was by a trusted friend before he came to know Dorothy as his birth-mother rather than as his 'adoptive' mother. In 1926 DLS married in a Registry Office a divorced war-veteran, 'Mac', whose children from his first marriage did not live with him.

Life was far from easy, what with the political and economic legacy of World War I to contend with, and the lack of sheer political will to make changes for the general good. Few could view the possibility of yet another major conflict with other than

1 In the selection Hone, R.E.(ed) *Poetry of Dorothy L. Sayers,* Dorothy L. Sayers Society, Swavesey, Cambridge, 1996, pp.78-79; and in Loades, A. (ed) *Dorothy L. Sayers. Spiritual Writings,* SPCK, London, 1993, pp.10-11 from her Opus 1.

the gravest misgivings. Yet it became imperative to destroy the 'Third Reich' with the consequences for the shape of post-war Europe emerging in the latter part of DLS' lifetime. She contributed vigorously to the thinking about the future which needed to be undertaken to bring about change both for the majority of the British population and for international relationships, not least those with defeated countries. Her detective fiction was by no means a trivial distraction from these important tasks, for in it she expressed some of her most passionately held convictions. For central to Christian faith is unequivocal commitment to truth and justice, without these being identified as specifically Christian in her novels. Thus when on honeymoon with Harriet (*Busman's Honeymoon* (1937) she and Peter together face the fact they cannot pick and choose, that they must have the truth no matter who suffers, and that nothing else matters. This will result in a death sentence for the murderer, and another agonising night for Peter as he waits for the eight a.m. moment of the execution, and who knows what consequences for others involved, however marginally. Human justice and the pursuit of truth will never be simple, and the aftermath unpredictable, hardly free of ambiguity and even of a measure of injustice. As Peter says, 'If there *is* a God or a judgement – what next? What have we done?'

God and judgement were precisely to become the focus of her attention when DLS was caught up into the orbit of Canterbury Cathedral and its Festival of Music and Drama. It was the 'drama' to be associated with the Festival which made it exceptional for its day, given the long-standing suspicion of the pre-Reformation traditions of theatre and liturgy almost wiped out by certain kinds of Protestantism. Canterbury happened to have as its Dean G.K.A. Bell, during the period when its Chapter (governing body) came to think it was time to challenge that suspicion. Having in 1927 founded the Friends of Canterbury Cathedral (an initiative to be followed in many other cathedrals) he found himself with an ally in the person of Margaret Babington, who became the Friends' Steward the following year. Chapter and Friends made possible plays

9

specially commissioned to be performed on the cathedral premises, continuing even after Bell has become Bishop of Chichester in 1929. [2] Bell remains important for understanding DLS' perspective on the cost of the Allied victory in World War II since he became a passionate critic of some aspects of the government's conduct of the war as an Episcopal member of the Upper House of Parliament (the 'Lords').

Both before and after Bell's time as Dean, the plays commissioned for Canterbury Cathedral were by a very distinguished lineage of writers, with T.S. Eliot's *Murder in the Cathedral* (1935) having a most profound impact, given that it was written for the Cathedral in which Thomas a` Becket had been done to death. It also reminded audiences of the possibility of continuing conflict between monarch/government and bishop. Following his own contribution on Thomas Cranmer, it was Charles Williams no less who suggested DLS as writer of a play for Canterbury, a choice not necessarily as surprising as some seem to have thought. She had some experience of stage performance and stagecraft from both school and university and a brief experience of school teaching. She had published a short 'poetic drama' *The Mocking of Christ* in her collection of *Catholic Tales and Christian Songs* (1918); *Busman's Honeymoon* had first seen the light of day as a play for the stage (1936), co-authored with another Somervillian, writer Muriel St Clare Byrne, distinguished historian and writer and lecturer at the Royal College of Dramatic Art, and one of DLS' valuable friends in the theatrical world. It was a singular challenge in itself to hit on a subject relevant to Canterbury, and this DLS triumphantly did in choosing to write about the rebuilding of the Cathedral Choir after the fire of 1174, chronicled by a monk, Gervase. Thus *The Zeal of Thy House* came into being, first performed between 12-18 June, 1937, in the Cathedral, and on a London stage in March 1938.

2. Jasper, R.C.D. *George Bell: Bishop of Chichester,* OUP, London, 1967. See also Pickering, K. *Drama in the Cathedral. The Canterbury Festival Plays 1928-1948* Churchman Publishing, Worthing, 1985.

In *Zeal,* some of DLS' convictions are made clear, notably in the character of the architect, William of Sens, the embodiment of the principal human sin, pride. The play is also significant for comprehending the significance for DLS of good work of whatever kind, and her grasp of what it means for human persons to acknowledge themselves as creative agents in the image of the divine Trinity. All this most painfully William has to learn. From this point on, some characteristic features of her work in drama began to emerge. Music specially written for her plays was integral to the liveliness of her presentation of Christian dogma, that in turn further heightened in some cases her scenes of debate and argument, testing vitally important judgements about the truth of a situation. Further, her new mode of success as a dramatist was in part the result of her personal humility, willing to take the expert advice of producers and actors as to what would and would not work 'on stage', however admirably written. She was always constructively involved in her productions, in every possible way, making 'cuts' as rehearsals proceeded, whilst frequently restoring her text for publication. Text not used in the original production might or might not be fruitfully used in subsequent ones, depending on context, which might be quite different from its first production.

Such was the success of *Zeal* that DLS was invited to write on Christian dogma for major newspapers, and in addition, received a commission from the then immensely prestigious BBC for a Nativity play (*He That Should Come*) to be broadcast on Christmas Day, 1938. It needs to be recalled that broadcasting was relatively new as a medium for large-scale communication to audiences, and the BBC had high expectations of what it should and should not present to its listeners. Of prime importance for DLS was that she conveyed to her listeners that Christ was born 'into the world', into 'real life', and she had to convey this by sound only. So she re-imagined the world into which Christ was born, engaging not merely with the relevant initial chapters of the first and third gospels (Matthew and Luke) but with centuries of

11

enjoyment of and reflection on the narratives and what had been perceived to be their significance. The main setting is the common courtyard of an inn, in which the characters DLS introduces can grumble about absolutely anything, with differing points of view to be expected from a Pharisee, a merchant and a centurion for example. Joseph plays a central role, and from the world beyond the courtyard the shepherds appear, and it is their gifts which are presented to the child newly born. Finally, we may note that as the published text of her Nativity play makes clear, DLS had not been intimidated by criticism that 'long speeches' would be unintelligible to her audiences, since she went on writing them, whilst allowing for them to be 'cut'. Much would depend on audiences and performers, and she had high expectations of all of them.

So successful was *He That Should Come* 'on air', indeed, that DLS was able to respond to a major challenge, namely, the writing of twelve radio plays (the first broadcast of which began on 21 December, 1941) entitled *The Man Born to be King*. These plays remain unique in their conception and execution, not least in wartime, and her vigorous introduction to the published version expounded her intentions as a writer in respect of 'the life of the God Incarnate' which gives us further insight into her theology. Christ 'on air' had to be credible, and so had the particular human beings with whom he had dealings, right through to the scenes when the risen Christ meets with his disciples, surely a major challenge for any dramatist. There were objections in advance of the broadcasts to listeners being able to hear the 'voice' of Jesus of Nazareth', but the fuss gave the plays excellent publicity, and they have remained a most moving exploration of the Gospels and their significance. Interestingly, given that she had limited the presence of the 'Kings' in *He That Should Come* to the 'Prologue' and the very last minutes of that play, in *The Man born to be King* she seized the opportunity further to explore their significance in the very first play of the twelve, 'Kings in Judea'.

That apart, there is an important thread of connection to notice which links DLS' exploration of the character of William in *Zeal* to the 1941 *The Man Born to be King*. William's principal sin was that of pride; that is also true of Judas according to her brilliant analysis and portrayal of him in *The Man Born to be King*. Between these two productions one further attempt to explore the roots of human sin in pride had presented itself in *The Devil to Pay*, first performed in Canterbury Cathedral 10-17 June, 1939, with a run on a London stage in the next month. (The outbreak of war in the first days of September was to cut short any further production at least for the time being). Writing this play may well have sharpened up DLS' perception of Judas and of Christ's dealings with him. The theme of *The Devil to Pay* is a re-working of the legend of Faustus- hardly easy to handle. In the first place it had no particular connection with Canterbury Cathedral. In the second place it could be very difficult to persuade an audience to take the 'devil' seriously as the personification of evil, for he was likely to be so entertaining as to 'upstage' the other characters, most importantly, that of Faustus with his besetting sin of pride. DLS had the courage to tackle the legend, because she saw in Faustus a figure which we might say was all too familiar in the political culture of her day, though she does not explicitly make the connection. For we can see behind her Faustus not just the 'impulsive reformer' in all his impatience, but the arrogance of the dictator who turns to unbridled violence as well as to fantasy, with incalculable harm as the result. Her attempt to tackle the full scope of Christ's atonement and redemption lay ahead of her, but there was at least one clue as to her confidence in print, for in her 1916 'The Gates of Paradise', DLS had written of the arrival of Judas accompanied by Christ himself at 'Hades gate' (alluding to the ancient tradition of Christ's raid upon those in bondage to Satan)[3]. It is important to bear this in mind to understand the final scene of *Devil*. Here she has Mephistopheles put in charge of the purging of Faustus and the destruction of the evil for which he has been responsible, but with Faustus himself secure

---

3. See Loades, *Dorothy L. Sayers. Spiritual Writings*, pp.12-15 from her Opus 1.

in the promise of his Judge that he will never be forsaken, and that he will be met by his Judge/Saviour at the gates of hell. DLS never denies the depths of human wickedness, but hangs on to a trust in 'redemption' on the very eve of war, of a scope and ferocity she and others at this stage could only fear.

In retrospect, it seems extraordinary, given the progress of World War II in its early stages, that anyone should have had the confidence to suppose that there should be serious consideration given to the shape of social and political life after the war, but to that consideration DLS indeed made a contribution. Thus, for example, in her essay in aesthetics and theology, her 1941 *The Mind of the Maker*, a major point is that if human dignity is to be respected, then social, political and economic life must be so ordered as to express human imagination and creativity. This conviction she spelled out in a series of notably pungent essays. Wartime, however, provoked her into writing one play with which she was richly satisfied, and that was to be *The Just Vengeance* of 1946. The maturity of her theological and dramatic vision now flowered in a play entirely original to herself, born of a number of factors. There was the stimulus Charles Williams' gave to her thinking with his 1943 *The Figure of Beatrice* (Williams himself sadly dying at the tail-end of the war). The result was her re-reading and translation of the whole of Dante's *Divine Comedy*, sometimes working away at this in air-raid shelters. And at this juncture DLS was presented with yet another opportunity to write for a Cathedral. In 1943 it was far from clear when the war might end, or on what terms, but the Chapter of Lichfield Cathedral had the vision and courage to advance plans for a service of Thanksgiving for the preservation of the Cathedral, and a Pageant to celebrate seven hundred and fifty years since its foundation, which fell in 1945. Given the inevitable austerities of wartime and its aftermath, it is unsurprising that the whole celebration could not take place in the anniversary year. The invitation to DLS to write a play for Lichfield gave her a priceless opportunity to relate Dante's vision to some deeply troubling features of her own era. (In addition to the play, her appropriation of Dante was to speak most powerfully to the reading public in the years after the war, made possible by the inclusion of her work on 'Hell' and 'Purgatory' in the new Penguin Classics series). It was in Canto xxi of 'Purgatory' that she found the phrase which became the title of *The Just Vengeance*, first performed June 15-26, 1946.

The importance of the phrase was to become clear as DLS wrote *The Just Vengeance*. No pacifist, she had come to the conclusion that the war simply had to be endured. That said, she and others had to reckon with a new dimension of war, which was the deliberate targeting of civilian populations from the air. As World War II developed, Bishop Bell for one became a serious critic of the policy which aimed at the systematic destruction of major German cities one by one, in order to bring the war to an end. For DLS there was a personal dimension to the matter of the bombing of civilians, however. She had learned much from Fraülein Fehmer, a music teacher at school, who had returned home to Frankfurt and become an ardent Nazi. DLS' poem 'Target Area' (1940) imagines her former teacher under the airborne onslaught, rightly recognising that in willing the war she willed the means, though their full horror was yet to be discovered. [4]

The issues she had to some extent explored in her detective fiction DLS now confronted in the light of Christian dogma, that is, that the divine court the human judges as well as the accused alike stand before God, that we are none of us free of guilt. Specifically in *The Just Vengeance* she set herself the task of portraying the Christian doctrine of redemption in the light of the conduct of the war. She set the action in a moment of time as an airman is shot down from his bomber, whilst drawing him into the whole company of those who have and continue to inhabit Lichfield. What she wanted above all to convey was what Dante himself had explored in his understanding of 'just vengeance' in the third and final 'Paradise' section of his *Comedy*. This is

4. Hone, *Poetry,* pp. 140-145.

that 'redemption', if embraced, leads the sanctified to experience the grace, joy and delight of salvation beyond agony and horror. This third section of Dante DLS knew very thoroughly, and drew on it throughout her play, though never completed her own translation and commentary on it before her own death in 1957. Thus *The Just Vengeance* yields irreplaceable insight into how she imagined the significance of 'redemption' for her own time. The popularity of 'Hell' in the immediate post-war period was understandable – the wicked getting their 'come-uppance' as it were; but the challenge of understanding 'redemption' was the greater. She rose to it magnificently, and was justifiably deeply satisfied with the result.

DLS by this time could draw on long-sustained friendships and trust with the professional actors and theatre people who had worked with her pre-war, with all involved surmounting the difficulties of securing and re-working needed materials in very short supply. Music was integral to the effectiveness of the production, and most fortunately she engaged the skills in costume and scene design of Norah Lambourne, with her extensive first-hand experience of theatre productions (in the 1950s crucial to the re-staging of the York Mystery Plays). She was also a key player in the production of DLS' final play, for another commemorative occasion. When Mac, DLS' husband died in 1950, Nora Lambourne moved in with DLS, becoming an invaluable collaborator for *The Emperor Constantine* first performed on Monday 2 July, 1951.

If writing a play for somewhere the size of Lichfield Cathedral was a challenge, an even more problematic context was the Colchester cinema in Festival of Britain year (1951) for Colchester's own festival contribution. The connection of Colchester with Constantine was through a legend which claimed that his mother, Helena, was the daughter of its King, Coel, DLS accepted no restrictions on the size of the cast, nor the time needed to perform the whole play (well over three hours), which displays the complexities of Constantine's achievement key, performed in London as *Christ's Emperor*. Like William of Sens, Judas, Faust and the bomber pilot, Constantine has most painfully to realise that the cleansing and redemption of his life comes about through Christ, and that is the precisely the consequence of the dogma he had been instrumental in establishing at Nicaea. It is his mother, Helena, who mediates this truth to him. The play may well be said to be of wider significance exhibiting the problems of connecting the dogmas of a church upheld by state authority, with political life and its associated miseries and triumphs. In its London context of St Thomas' Church off Regent Street the shorter version (*Christ's* Emperor) was set for a challenging run, but the death of George VI in its very first week put paid to it. Age-old issues about the human pursuit of truth and justice all too evidently remain.

DLS' work in many genres continued until her unexpected death in 1957. It is thanks to the initiative of Wipf & Stock that we have the texts of these six productions re-published in single volume format, sponsored by the Dorothy L. Sayers Society. Everyone owes an inestimable debt to Dr Barbara Reynolds, engaged life-long with the work of Dante, with DLS' appropriation of Dante, completing the 'Paradise' section of the *Comedy* after DLS' death, editing her letters, writing her biography, and in so many ways stimulating interest in the whole range of work of a most remarkable human being.

The 'religious' plays of DLS, devised for cathedrals, stages and broadcasts were written to be adaptable for performance in many different contexts. They are meant to be exciting, stirring, challenging, memorable, getting everyone involved at the most serious level with issues of inescapable and permanent importance.

Ann Loades
Tayport, Scotland
April 2011

Synopses of the Religious Drama by Dorothy Sayers

THE ZEAL OF THY HOUSE

Dorothy L. Sayers took her inspiration from a monk's account of the fire of 1174, and the subsequent rebuilding of Canterbury Cathedral Quire. She portrays William of Sens, the chosen architect, as eaten away by pride in his splendid work, unable to give glory to God for his achievement. Enacted in the presence of a group of graciously influential Archangels, the play reveals the carelessness of some of the monks, resulting in the terrifying fall that cripples William. His agony brings him to repentance and gratitude before God, and finally to the renunciation of his role, leaving the completion of the re-building to others.

First performed on June 12, 1937; first published by V. Gollancz in June 1937.

HE THAT SHOULD COME

In this first of her plays for religious broadcasting, Dorothy L. Sayers wanted to convince listeners of the truth that Christ was born into our deeply problematic world, in his case, in territory overrun by an army of occupation. Although framed as it were by the voices of the three 'wise men' asking whether the birth of a particular child could possibly fulfil their desires, the focus of the play is on the conflict of opinion (about roads, taxes, and so forth) expressed by those in the courtyard of the inn at Bethlehem. Joseph is given a most significant role, and it is the shepherds whose gifts are presented when the Holy Family is revealed.

First broadcast on December 25, 1938; first published by V. Gollancz in November 1939.

THE DEVIL TO PAY

Dorothy L. Sayers re-worked the legend of Faust as a serious 'comedy', presenting Faust as one who chooses wicked means as an end to an admirable goal: the relief of suffering (while becoming entirely focussed on his own supposed satisfactions). In the last scene, in the Court of Heaven, Azrael, angel of the souls of the dead, claims Faustus' soul, opposing Mephistopheles' claim. With the knowledge of good and evil returned to him, Faustus finally accepts that his evil must be cleansed, with Mephistopheles serving as the agent of that purgation. Faustus accepts his need for cleansing, trusting that the divine Judge/Court President, will indeed in mercy meet him at the very gates of hell, finally redeemed.

First performed on June 10, 1939; first published by V. Gollancz in June 1939.

THE MAN BORN TO BE KING

In twelve plays for broadcasting at monthly intervals, Dorothy L. Sayers drew on material from all four Gospels, keeping the theme of Jesus of Nazareth's divine kingship in focus throughout, while locating him firmly in the social and political context of his time. The first half cover episodes that precede the final journey to Jerusalem and the latter half primarily deal with Passion Week themes. It is on the simplicity and profundity of Jesus' words in the Fourth Gospel especially that Sayers drew on in her own writing for the 'voice' of Jesus 'on air'. The plays gave her an opportunity to explore the many gospel characters surrounding Jesus, not least that of Judas. And beyond the utter sorrow of Jesus' death, the King comes into his own in the garden of resurrection.

The first play was broadcast on December 21, 1941, with the rest at four-weekly intervals thereafter, concluding on October 18, 1942; first published by V. Gollancz in 1943.

THE JUST VENGEANCE

In this play Dorothy L. Sayers addressed the crimes and problems of human life, especially those of the victors in war,

19

in an entirely novel way, by precipitating an airman in the very moment of his death back into the company of citizens of the 'City', in this case, Lichfield. The citizens range from Adam and Eve (Adam himself the inventor of the axe which kills Abel) together with other biblical characters in the history of redemption brought to new life as members of the City, (e.g. Judas is a common informer). Others bear burdens of shame, toil, fear, poverty and ingratitude. Former inhabitants (e.g. George Fox, Dr. Johnson) help the airman to see that no more than they can he shift the burden of his guilt and grief that they all share. There is but one remedy, to join the 'Persona Dei' carrying his cross, finding indeed that he bears their burdens for them. The 'Persona Dei' is finally seen in resurrection and glory.

First performed on June 15, 1946; first published by V. Gollancz in June 1946. Broadcast: March 30, 1947.

THE EMPEROR CONSTANTINE

A brief 'Prologue' by the 'Church' introduces the career of Constantine (from A.D. 305-337) with scenes from the empires of both west and east, concentrating on Constantine's progress to imperial power and inevitably in religious belief. He discovers Christ to be the God who has made him his earthly vice-regent as single Emperor. Summoning the Council of Nicaea at 325, an invigorating debate results in the acceptance of Constantine's formula that Christ is 'of one substance with God'. The implications of the creed of Nicaea are revealed in the last part of the play in which it is his mother, Helena, who brings him to the realisation that he needs redemption by Christ for his political and military life as well as for the domestic tragedy which has resulted in the death of his son.

First performed on July 2, 1951; first published by V. Gollancz in August 1951. A shortened version entitled *Christ's Emperor* was performed at St Thomas' Church, Regent Street in February 1952.

Latin Texts in The Zeal of Thy House

This material is taken from *The Zeal of Thy House*, the edition with Preface and Notes by C.H.Rieu, London: Methuen & Co Ltd. 36 Essex Street London WC2 (1961). *Appendix Three* Translations of Latin Hymns and Prayers, by C. H. Rieu, p.81-84.

p.24, **O quanta qualia**

There dawns no Sabbath, no Sabbath is o'er,
Those Sabbath-keepers have one evermore;
One and unending is that triumph-song
Which to the Angels and us shall belong.
(Verses 1,3,5 of the hymn by Peter Abelard,
1079-1142, translated by J.M. Neale,
English Hymnal No 465.)
Also to be found as No. 432 of The New English Hymnal.

p.72 **O felix culpa. . . .**

O happy fault, which has deserved to have
such and so mighty a Redeemer.
(From the "Exultet" of the Roman Liturgy for Holy Saturday.)

pp.86-87 **Sancta Maria, ora pro nobis. . . .**

Holy Mary, pray for us;
Holy Mother of God, pray for us;
Holy Virgin of Virgins, pray for us;
Mother most chaste, pray for us;
Mother inviolate, pray for us;
Mother unstained, pray for us;

Virgin to be venerated, pray for us;
Virgin to be proclaimed, pray for us;
Virgin most mighty, pray for us;

Vessel meet to be honoured, pray for us;
Wondrous vessel of devotion, pray for us;
Mystic Rose, pray for us;

Tower of David, pray for us;
Tower of ivory, pray for us;
House of God, pray for us.
(From the Roman Liturgy of the Blessed Virgin.)

p.88 **Agnus Dei,. . . .**

Lamb of God, that takest away the sins of
The world, spare us, O Lord;. . . hear us,
O Lord; . . . have mercy on us.
(From the Mass.)

p.99-100 **Plebs angelica, ...**

Angelic host,
Phalanx and squadron of the Prince-Archangels,
Uranian power,
Strength of the gracious word,

Spirits that have dominion, Cherubim
Divine tribunal of the air,
And Seraphim with flaming hair,

And you, O Michael, Prince of Heaven,
And Gabriel, by whom the word was given,

And Raphael, born in the house of life,
Bring us among the folk of Paradise.

(Fragment of a sequence in honour of St.
Michael, from a tenth-century tropa of St.
Martial of Limoges. English translation by
Helen Waddell. Music composed in 1944
for the Choir of Camterbury Cathedral by
Michael Tippett, and first performed on 6th
August 1944.)

p.110 O lux beata trinitas. . . .

O Trinity, most Blessed light,
O Unity of primal Might,
As now the fiery sun departs,
Shed Thou Thy beams within our hearts.

To Thee our morning song of praise,
To Thee our evening prayer we raise;
Thee may our heart and voice adore
For ever and for evermore.

(From the Latin hymn of St Ambrose (A.D. 340-397),
translated by J.M.Neale. English Hymnal No.164.)
Also to be found as No. 54 of The New English Hymnal.

pp.118-119 Quantus tremor est futurus. . . .

O, what fear man's bosom rendeth,
When from heaven the Judge descendeth,
On whose sentence all dependeth.

Wondrous sound the trumpet flingeth,
Through earth's sepulchres it ringeth,
All before the throne it bringeth.

Lo! The book exactly worded,
Wherein all hath been recorded;
Thence shall judgement be awarded.

What shall I, frail man, be pleading?
Who for me be interceding,
When the just are mercy needing?

(Requiem Mass Sequence from the poem
known as *Dies Irae* (Day of Wrath, or Judgement) by
Thomas of Celano, *c.*1250,
Translated by W.J. Irwin. English Hymnal No.351.)
Also to be found as No. 524 of The New English Hymnal.

p.125 Faithful Cross. . . .

Part of the Office Hymn for Passion Sunday,
by Bishop Venantius Fortunatus, A.D. 530-609,

translated by J.M. Neale, English Hymnal No.96.)
Another translation of this hymn (by Percy Dearmer)
is to be found in The New English Hymnal No.517.

p.129-130 **O Quanta qualia. . . .**

Oh, what the joy and the glory must be,
Those endless Sabbaths the blessed ones see;
Crown for the valiant, for weary ones rest;
God shall be All and in all ever blest.

Truly Jerusalem name we that shore,
Vision of peace, that brings joy evermore;
Wish and fulfilment can sever'd be never,
Nor the thing pray'd for come short of the prayer.

There dawns no Sabbath, no Sabbath is o'er,
Those Sabbath-keepers have one evermore;
One and unending is that triumph-song
Which to the Angels and us shall belong.

(Verses 1,3,5 of the hymn by Peter Abelard,
1079-1142, translated by J.M. Neale, English Hymnal No. 465.)
Also to be found as No. 432 of The New English Hymnal.

PREFACE

A schoolboy, asked to state what he knew of Mary Tudor, replied: " She was known as Bloody Mary but she was not half as bloody as you'd think."

We might reasonably expect Miss Sayers, since the previous plays written or performed at the invitation of the Friends of Canterbury Cathedral have concerned prelates and kings who have come to violent and untimely ends, to write with relish of archbishops and assassination, for she has already proved herself to be thoroughly at home with peers and homicide. But, like Mary Tudor, she has not fulfilled our sanguine expectations. Many will be relieved to find that her hero is an architect, that such violence as there may be is accidental, and that, though a rope is the instrument of his downfall, it is accessory to a windlass and not to a gallows.

At a time when all works of fiction are prefaced by a passionate declaration that the author's characters are entirely imaginary, it is a pleasant change to have to vouch for the authenticity of the main protagonists in this play. It is true that, while most people are familiar with the names of those who damaged or were murdered in Canterbury Cathedral, William of Sens, who designed and built the greater part of it, is not as well known as he ought to be. When the choir was burnt down in 1174, he was chosen by a nervous Chapter to undertake the work of reconstruction. Then as now, that a foreigner in competition with native contractors should be selected for such a task must have caused furious comment. Nevertheless, in the face of official timidity and practical obstacles, he succeeded in raising from the ashes of Lanfranc's work the leaping choir which we cherish to-day. This creation, magnificent as it is, might hardly seem to be suitable material for a dramatic work. But Miss Sayers chooses William of Sens to be the vehicle for her theme of the artist who in the supreme moment of mastery over his craft may be thrown

25

down and destroyed by a consuming and wasting infirmity, the germ of which is in us all and which too often, fostered by our unawareness, destroys virtue and vitality with its insidious infection. Though few may have fallen physically as far and as hard as William, many have fallen away artistically and have perished without the revelation which was granted to him.

The only scenes which may be suspect historically are those between William and the Lady Ursula. It might be considered a little unfair to credit William with an imaginary intrigue; but, in fact, Miss Sayers has ingenious and moderately sound reasons for doing so.

Our authority for these events is the contemporary chronicle of Gervase the Monk. After recording with horror and enthusiasm the fire and the rebuilding, he refers to William's accident in a strange and pregnant sentence; he attributes the calamity to " either the Vengeance of God or the Envy of the Devil." Can we not detect in this the verdict of one who, while full of admiration for the Master's work, has watched with disapproval, and not a little envy, the pride and license which the artist has been at little pains to conceal, and now records a well-merited if lamented punishment with righteous satisfaction ? Herein may be the clue to some such fall from grace as that which Miss Sayers suggests in the scenes between the architect and his admirer.

For the rest the play deals with well-established facts. Avoiding sham archaism and the fusty language which is too often expected and provided in plays of period, it presents the Middle Ages as being very little removed in essentials from our own. Petrol and patent medicines have taken the place of the windlass and the faith-healing of the pilgrims, but human fallibility and the inspiration of the artist remain constant. The Archangels who from time to time descend into the arena and direct the destinies of the groundlings need not bewilder the reader or the spectator. They represent the Will of God, Fate, Providence, Accident or what you will and, in the final scenes, that bright flash of intuition which occasionally illuminates even the most clouded conscience.

LAURENCE IRVING

THE ZEAL OF THY HOUSE was written for presentation by the Friends of Canterbury Cathedral, and was first acted in the Chapter House at the Canterbury Festival, 12th–18th June, 1937, with Mr. Harcourt Williams as William of Sens and a mixed cast of professional and amateur performers.

It was first presented in London by Mr. Anmer Hall at the Westminster Theatre, on 29th March, 1938, with Mr. Harcourt Williams, Mr. Frank Napier and Mr. Michael Gough in their original parts, and with the original music and costumes.

Mr. Williams and Mr. Napier were the producers on both occasions. The special music was composed by Mr. Gerald H. Knight, the Cathedral Organist at Canterbury.

The present text is that of the play as first written. At Canterbury, it was presented without interval, and in a slightly shortened form. In London, an interval was found necessary between Parts II and III, and the following chorus was accordingly inserted at the beginning of Part III:

The Lord God of Heaven hath given me all the kingdoms of the earth; and He hath charged me to build Him an house at Jerusalem.

That every man should eat and drink and enjoy the good of all his labour, it is the gift of God.

Not unto us, O Lord, not unto us, but unto Thy name give the praise;

For we look for a city which hath foundations, whose builder and maker is God.

The only other modification of any importance was in St. Michael's final speech, the last sentences of which were altered as follows:

Behold, then, and honour, all beautiful work of the craftsman, imagined by men's minds, built by the labour of men's hands, working with power upon the souls of men, image of the everlasting Trinity, God's witness in world and time.

And whatsoever ye do, do all to the Glory of God.

With the help of these modifications, the play in its original form should prove sufficiently elastic to adapt itself for production in any theatre or place of public or private performance.

DOROTHY L. SAYERS

DRAMATIS PERSONÆ

Angelic Persons:

MICHAEL ⎫
RAPHAEL ⎬ Archangels
GABRIEL ⎭

CASSIEL, the Recording Angel
A YOUNG CHERUB, Thurifer to Raphael

Religious:

THE PRIOR OF CHRISTCHURCH ⎫
STEPHEN, the Treasurer │
THEODATUS, the Sacristan │ Choir
MARTIN, the Guest-Brother and Infirmarian │ Brothers
AMBROSE, the Choirmaster │ and
WULFRAM, the Director of the Farm ⎬ members
ERNULPHUS, the Director of the Kitchen and │ of the
    Distillery │ Cathedral
PAUL, the Gardener │ Chapter
HILARY, the Almoner │
SILVESTER, the Painter │
GERVASE, the Historian and Clerk ⎭

HUBERT, an Oblate, Superintendent of the Rough Masons

Laymen:

WILLIAM OF SENS, Architect to the Cathedral

JOHN OF KENT ⎫
HENRY OF YORK ⎬ Rival Architects

SIMON ⎫
WALTER │
HUGH ⎬ Workmen
GEOFFREY ⎭

A YOUNG BOY
THE LADY URSULA DE WARBOIS
Monks; Lay-Brothers; Workmen; Pilgrims of both sexes

Two Cantors and a Choir of Mixed Voices

———

The action takes place during the years 1175–1179.

NOTE.—The names Michaël, Raphaël, are to be pronounced as
    trisyllables throughout.

I

At the opening of the play, the scene is set as for a meeting of the Chapter, with seats about a long table. The CHOIR *having entered and taken their places, they sing the hymn following:*

CHOIR

Disposer supreme, and judge of the earth,
Thou choosest for Thine the weak and the poor;
To frail earthen vessels and things of no worth
Entrusting Thy riches which aye shall endure.

Those vessels soon fail, though full of Thy light,
And at Thy decree are broken and gone;
Then brightly appeareth the arm of Thy might,
As through the clouds breaking the lightnings have
shone.

[During the singing of the second half of this verse, there enter MICHAEL, RAPHAEL *with his* THURIFER, GABRIEL *and* CASSIEL *the Recorder. They pass slowly to the steps while the next verse is sung.*

Like clouds are they borne to do Thy great will,
And swift as the wind about the world go;
All full of Thy Godhead while earth lieth still,
They thunder, they lighten, the waters o'erflow.

℣. He maketh His angels spirits.
℟. And His ministers a flaming fire.

MICHAEL

I am God's servant Michael the Archangel;
I walk in the world of men invisible,
Bearing the sword that Christ bequeathed His Church
To sunder and to save.

RAPHAEL

I am God's servant
Raphael the Archangel; and I walk
In the world of men invisible; I receive
Prayer spoken or unspoken, word or deed
Or thought or whatsoever moves the heart,
Offering it up before the Throne.

GABRIEL

I am
God's servant the Archangel Gabriel,
The heavenly runner between God and man,
Moving invisible.

CASSIEL

God's Recorder, I,
That keep the Book and cast up all accounts,
Cassiel, chief scrivener to the Courts of Heaven.

℣. Their sound is gone out into all lands.
℟. And their words into the ends of the world.

[*During the singing of the following verse, the* ANGELIC
PERSONS *depart severally,* MICHAEL *standing above* RAPHAEL
on the right side of the steps, and the THURIFER *kneeling below
them;* CASSIEL *with his book on the left side of the steps with*
GABRIEL *above.*

CHOIR

Oh, loud be Thy trump and stirring the sound,
To rouse us, O Lord, from sin's deadly sleep;
May lights which Thou kindlest in darkness around
The dull soul awaken her vigils to keep.

[*The Recorder*, CASSIEL, *sits at his desk;*

RAPHAEL *hands his censer to the* THURIFER, *and sits.*

MICHAEL

What is our business here to-day in Canterbury?
CASSIEL (*slapping the Book rather sharply open and running his finger down the page*)
A meeting of the Cathedral Chapter to choose an architect for the rebuilding of the Choir after the great fire of 1174.

RAPHAEL (*reminiscently*)

Ah, yes—the choir. I was sorry to see the old one go. It was very beautiful, and a favourite haunt of mine. Prayer had soaked into the stones and sanctified them.

CASSIEL (*austerely*)

Mankind are exceedingly careless of their possessions. I have an entry against one Tom Hogg, neatherd, who neglected to clean his chimney and so had his thatch set on fire. The sparks were blown across the road and lodged under the lead roof of the church. In a short time all was ablaze.

GABRIEL

A heavy consequence for a light offence. Was that your doing, Michael?

MICHAEL

It was. I bore the flame betwixt my hands and set it among the rafters. We fanned it with our wings, my angels and I, riding upon the wind from the south.

CASSIEL (*muttering to himself over the Book*)

. . . and seven, twenty-six . . . and three, twenty-nine . . . and nine, thirty-eight. . . .

RAPHAEL

Was it done to avenge the murder of the Archbishop ?

CASSIEL

. . . and six. Put down four and carry eight.

MICHAEL

I do not know. I am a soldier. I take my orders.

CASSIEL (*casting up a column and ruling a line beneath it*)

We all do that, Michael. Your interference in the matter does not affect the debit against Tom Hogg. He stands charged with Sloth to a considerable amount. What use was made of his sin is neither here nor there. It is a question of economics.

MICHAEL

Quite so. I could have done the work perfectly well myself, with a thunderbolt. Hogg's sin was not in the least necessary.

GABRIEL (*in humorous resignation*)

Nothing that men do is ever necessary. At least, that is my experience. I find them very amusing.

[*The sound of the " Veni Creator " is heard from the lower end of the Chapter-House as the* CHOIR-MONKS *enter in procession.*

RAPHAEL

I find them very pathetic.

GABRIEL

You see them at their best, Raphael; as Michael sees them at their worst.

MICHAEL

I find them very perverse. If God were not infinite, they would surely exhaust His patience.

CASSIEL

They make a great deal of work in the counting house. Happily, being an angel, and not a man, I like work. The hatred of work must be one of the most depressing consequences of the Fall.

GABRIEL

Some men work like angels—and whistle over their work. They are much the most cheerful kind.

[*In the meantime,* RAPHAEL *has met the* MONKS *at the foot of the steps and now precedes them to the Chapter, swinging his censer before them. The last verse of the hymn is sung by the* MONKS *standing about the table. Then all sit.* RAPHAEL *comes down to sit beside* MICHAEL. CASSIEL *opens the Book at a fresh page and prepares to take minutes of the meeting.*

PRIOR

Brethren, the business before us is, as you know, the appointment of an architect for the new choir. Our earlier discussions have brought the number of suitable candidates down to three. To-day we have to make our final choice.

THEODATUS

Under God's guidance.

PRIOR

Under God's guidance, of course, Father Theodatus. The three men in question are John of Kent, William of Sens, and Henry of York.

STEPHEN

Have we got the estimates, Father Prior?

PRIOR (*handing papers to* STEPHEN)

I have two of them here. Henry of York's is lower than John of Kent's. He thinks he can restore the existing fabric without pulling it all down and rebuilding.

WULFRAM

Will that be safe? Some of the masonry looks to me very insecure. John of Kent is a local man—he has had more opportunity to judge. Besides, it would look well to give the work to a local man.

ERNULPHUS

John is very young—young men are always full of extravagant ideas. No experience.

HILARY

One must encourage young men. The future is with the young.

STEPHEN

John's estimate is certainly rather high. I don't think we can countenance extravagance.

PRIOR

We must consider expense, of course, Father Treasurer. Perhaps we had better have the architects in and hear what they have to say. Father Gervase—if you will be so good——

[GERVASE *goes out by door, right.*

AMBROSE

Speaking as Choirmaster, may I urge here and now that we should get a man who understands something about acoustics. The old choir——

PAUL

What we want is the old choir restored to what it was before. I dislike this trivial modern stuff they are putting up all over the place, with its pointed arcading and flourishy capitals. Give me something solid, like Ely.

HILARY

One must move with the times, Father Paul. Now William of Sens is a progressive man.

WULFRAM

He is a foreigner. Why should we have a foreigner? Isn't an Englishman good enough? Money should be kept in the country.

STEPHEN

We do not seem to have had an estimate from William of Sens.

[*Re-enter* GERVASE *right with* JOHN OF KENT, WILLIAM OF SENS, *and* HENRY OF YORK.

PRIOR

Not yet. He writes to me here—— Ah, good morning, sirs. Pray come to the table. We have received your letters and considered your qualifications. We are now minded to hear your further opinions, after inspection of the site. You, Master Henry, have submitted a very conservative estimate of the cost of reconstruction.

HENRY

My Lord Prior, I have kept the expense down to the lowest possible figure; and after examination of the standing masonry I have prepared a plan and elevation.

[*Producing it.*

PRIOR

Let us have that.

[HENRY *puts the plan before the* PRIOR *and moves across to left of table.*

HENRY

You will see that I have allowed for keeping the greater part of the standing fabric. (THEODATUS *and* ERNULPHUS on PRIOR's *left examine the plan.*) With the exception of the more grievously damaged portions which I have marked, I see no reason why the present structure may not be restored——

[*He passes plan down to the* MONKS, *on left.*

JOHN

My Lord Prior——

HENRY

—and put into good order along the original lines. The existing outer walls may be retained——

WULFRAM

You think they are not too much weakened by the action of the fire ?

JOHN

Weakened ? They are calcined in places almost to powder.

HENRY

They can be patched and grouted, Master John; and by the addition of supporting buttresses and by altering the pitch of the roof so as to lessen the thrust——

SILVESTER (*who has been studying the plan with* MARTIN)

Will not the effect of the buttresses be somewhat clumsy ?

MARTIN

There is something a little mean in the proportions of this roof.

AMBROSE (*who is a man of one idea*)

I should think it would be bad for sound. After all, the chief use of a choir is to hold services in.

MARTIN

The sooner we get *a* choir the better. The singing has been very bad lately. I am ashamed to hear sacred words so howled.

[*Hands back plan to* HENRY, *who takes it across, right, to* WULFRAM.

AMBROSE (*defensively*)

The nave is very awkward to sing in. What with the west end boarded up——

BH

HILARY

Well, we can't be expected to hold our services in full view, not to say smell, of the common people.

AMBROSE

And the east end boarded up——

[ERNULPHUS *quietly falls asleep.*

WULFRAM (*taking plan*)

The draughts are appalling. I caught a shocking cold last Tuesday.

AMBROSE

We are singing in a wooden box. You can't sing properly in a box.

PRIOR

Time is certainly of some importance.

STEPHEN

The cost is still more important.

HENRY (*moving up again left of table*)

To repair, according to my plan, will be very much cheaper and quicker than to pull down and rebuild. I could engage to be ready within two years——

JOHN

And in two years more you will have to rebuild again. My Lord Prior——

PRIOR

You, Master John, recommend a complete reconstruction ?

JOHN

Recommend? It must be done. Do not be deceived. This botching is useless and dangerous. It is unworthy——

HENRY

Master John, I am older than you and more experienced——

JOHN

You never in your life built anything bigger than a parish church.

PRIOR

Master John, Master John!

JOHN

This is the Cathedral Church of Christ at Canterbury. It must be the wonder of the realm—nay, of the world! Will you insult God with patchwork? Give me the commission, Lord Prior, and I will build you a church worth looking at!

[*Producing plan and elevation, which he passes to* STEPHEN.

HENRY

To the greater glory of Master John of Kent!

JOHN

To the glory of God and of the blessed Saints Dunstan and Elphege.

STEPHEN (*aside to the* PRIOR)

And the entire depletion of the Treasury. Will somebody please tell me where the money is to come from?

THEODATUS

The devotion of the common people is most touching. A poor widow yesterday brought us five farthings, all her little savings.

STEPHEN

Our Lord will reward her. But that will not go very far.

MARTIN

I think we ought to take the long view. Canterbury is the most important church in the Kingdom, and attracts a great many people to the town. What with the visitors and the great increase in the number of pilgrims since the lamented death of the late Archbishop——

ALL

Blessed St. Thomas, pray for us.

[*They cross themselves.*

MARTIN

A little money spent now on building will repay itself handsomely in donations and bequests.

[STEPHEN *passes the plan to* HILARY.

THEODATUS (*rather loudly*)

If the fire was a Divine judgment for the Archbishop's murder——

ERNULPHUS (*waking with a start*)

Eh ? the Archbishop ? Blessed St. Thomas, pray for us.

[*He crosses himself and falls asleep instantly.*

THEODATUS

I say, if the fire was a judgment, then the new building is a reparation to God, and should be an offering worthy of its high destination and a sufficient sacrifice for the sins of this country.

SILVESTER

No artist can do his best work when he has to consider every halfpenny. Thou shalt not muzzle the ox——

THEODATUS

All this talk about money is sheer lack of faith. God will provide.

STEPHEN

No doubt. But, humanly speaking, the accounts will have to go through the Treasury, and I feel responsible.

HILARY (*passing design to* PAUL)

There is a good deal of elaborate and expensive ornament here, Master John.

PAUL

Modern nonsense, modern nonsense. Let us have the old choir back. Here is a groined roof and a clerestory and a lot of fiddle-faddle. How long is all this going to take ?

JOHN (*uncompromisingly*)

Seven years—perhaps more.

MARTIN

Seven years ! Have we to put up with half a cathedral for seven years ? Why, God made the world in six days !

41

PRIOR

God, Father Martin, was not subject to limitations of funds or material.

JOHN (*angrily aside to* WILLIAM)

Nor to the cheese-paring parsimony of a monastic chapter.

WILLIAM (*who has listened to all this with a quiet smile; with a touch of humour*)

Possibly God is an abler architect than any of us.

PRIOR

We have not yet heard your opinion, Master William. Do you think it possible to restore the remaining fabric ?

WILLIAM

Oh, I should think very likely. I should certainly hope to save some of it.

JOHN (*angrily to* WILLIAM)

That is *not* what you said to us outside.

WILLIAM

But I really cannot say—I do not see how anybody can say—without prolonged and careful examination.

AMBROSE

That's very true. Very reasonable.

WILLIAM

That is why I have as yet prepared no estimate or plan. But I have brought some drawings of the work entrusted

to me at Sens and elsewhere which will give you some idea
of the kind of thing I should like to do here.

[*Hands papers to* PRIOR.

PRIOR

Now, I like that. Extremely fine and dignified. And very
modern in feeling.

STEPHEN

And not too ornate.

[WILLIAM *hands them on down right.*

GERVASE

It is wonderful. It is like a poem in stone. I should dearly
love to see it. How light—and yet how majestic !

[*He looks admiringly at* WILLIAM.

WILLIAM

Time and cost would depend on the extent of the work.
I suggest making a thorough survey before getting out a
preliminary plan and estimate. Naturally, I should
commit you to nothing without the advice and approval
of yourself, Lord Prior and the Father Treasurer.

STEPHEN

Just so. We should object to nothing in reason.

WILLIAM (*he has now got the ear of the house*)

I should be obliged (*firmly*) to stipulate for the best
materials.

THEODATUS

God's service demands the best materials.

WILLIAM

But we can effect an economy by making good use of

local talent, of which I am sure we must possess a great deal——

WULFRAM

I am all in favour of local talent.

WILLIAM

And we may reduce the cost of shipping and carriage by the use of certain mechanical devices of my own invention, which I need not say I shall be happy to place at the disposal of the authorities without extra fee.

PRIOR

Thank you—that is very proper, very generous. . . . H'm. Well, Brethren, I think we have now the facts before us. If these gentlemen would kindly retire for a few moments. . . .

[General movement, GERVASE *goes up, right, to door.*

ERNULPHUS *(waking with a start)*

Eh, what ? what ? Have we finished ?

SILVESTER

No, Father Ernulphus. The architects are retiring while we deliberate.

ERNULPHUS

Oh, I see. Very good.

[He falls asleep again.

HENRY

Two or three years only, Lord Prior—say four at most—and a strict regard for economy.

[Exit HENRY.

JOHN

Consider, Lord Prior—a structure worthy of its dedication —and safety to life and limb, if you think that matters.

[*Exit* JOHN.

WILLIAM

Sir, if I am chosen, I will do my best.

[*Exit* WILLIAM. GERVASE *follows them off. The rest examine the plans and documents.*

GABRIEL

The motives of mankind are lamentably mixed.

RAPHAEL

They mean well, I assure you.

MICHAEL

Then it is a pity they do not say what they mean.

CASSIEL

It is most confusing. I have worn out my pen trying to keep up with them.

GABRIEL

That is easily remedied. Allow me.

[*He plucks a feather from his own wing and hands it to* CASSIEL *as* GERVASE *re-enters and shuts the door.*

CASSIEL (*trimming the feather into a pen*)

Thank you.

PRIOR

Well, Brethren ?

SILVESTER

I must say, Master Henry's plan seems rather make-shift.

45

WULFRAM

He is a Yorkshire man. I would as soon have a foreigner as a Yorkshire man.

STEPHEN

He is too anxious to please. First he says two years—then three or four. I should not rely on his estimate.

PRIOR

Are we agreed, then, not to appoint Henry of York? (*The* MONKS *signify agreement.*) Then that leaves us the choice between John of Kent and William of Sens.

MICHAEL

What will they make of that?

CASSIEL

They will choose the man whom God has appointed.

GABRIEL

I shall see to it that they do.

WULFRAM

Let us have John. He is a local man.

[*As the* MONKS *give their votes,* GERVASE *notes them down.*

MARTIN

Yes; his church will attract attention and bring people into the town.

PAUL

Too new-fangled and showy. I am for William. I distrust these go-ahead young men.

HILARY

I have said William all along.

GERVASE

Clearly William is a great craftsman—let us choose him.

THEODATUS

We know nothing about him personally. John is a young man of devout life.

STEPHEN

What has that to do with it? Besides, his manners are abominable. I give my voice for William.

SILVESTER

I like John's plan—we haven't seen William's.

AMBROSE

John's plan looks good from the musician's point of view.

PRIOR

I must not influence you—but I admit I am greatly impressed by William of Sens. . . . Father Gervase, how does the voting stand?

GERVASE

Five have spoken for John and five for William.

GABRIEL

This is where I interfere.

[*He goes up into the Chapter-House.*

PRIOR

Somebody has not voted. Who is it?

[*Everybody stares round at* ERNULPHUS.

MARTIN

It is Father Ernulphus.

THEODATUS

He has been asleep all the time.

[GABRIEL *stands behind* ERNULPHUS.

PAUL

He is getting very shaky, poor old soul.

THEODATUS *(loudly in* ERNULPHUS' *ear)*

Father Ernulphus !

ERNULPHUS *(starting into consciousness)*

Eh ? eh ? what ?

THEODATUS *(shouting in his ear)*

Do you vote for John of Kent or William of Sens ?

GABRIEL *(in his other ear)*

William of Sens.

ERNULPHUS *(to* THEODATUS)

Eh ? Yes, of course. William of Sens. Certainly.

[*He closes his eyes again.*

THEODATUS *(vexed)*

He hasn't heard a word. *(Loudly)* Father Ernulphus !

ERNULPHUS *(suddenly alert)*

You needn't shout. I'm not deaf. I have followed everything very carefully. I said William of Sens and I mean
William of Sens.

[*He shuts his eyes tight with an air of finality.*

THEODATUS

Really, Father Prior !

You will never move him now.

[A pause.

PRIOR

The vote of the Chapter, then, is for William of Sens. If there is no further business, the Chapter is dissolved.

ALL (*rising*)

Glory be to the Father, and to the Son, and to the Holy Ghost. As it was in the beginning, is now and ever shall be, world without end. Amen.

[GABRIEL *goes up and stands above.*

PRIOR (*as the* MONKS *begin to file down, left and right*)

Father Gervase, pray inform the architects of this decision. Thank those that are not chosen for their pains; they shall receive their journey-money from the Father Treasurer. Ask Master William to come and see me. No time must be lost in putting the work in hand, for the night cometh wherein no man can work.

[*Exit* GERVASE, *right, as the* PRIOR *follows the* MONKS *out.*

℣. Be strong, all ye people of the land, saith the Lord, and work; for I am with you, saith the Lord God of Hosts.

℞. No man, having put his hand to the plough, and looking back, is fit for the Kingdom of God.

℣. There is nothing better than that a man should rejoice in his own works, for that is his portion.

℞. Ascribe ye greatness unto our God; He is the Rock, His work is perfect.

[*Re-enter* GERVASE, *right, with* JOHN, HENRY *and* WILLIAM.

JOHN (*indignantly to* WILLIAM)

Trickery, Master William, sheer trickery and cheating. You know well enough that you *cannot* restore a single stone of it.

HENRY (*with equal indignation*)

You will tell any lie in order to get the job. You promise economy, and you will spend their money like water. It is treacherous—it is dishonest——

WILLIAM

You would not only promise, you would *do* them a dishonest piece of work. *That* is treachery, if you like, Master Henry.

[HENRY *bounces down the steps with an angry exclamation.*

JOHN

But why must you flatter and fawn on them ? Why pander to all their ridiculous foibles ? Cannot you tell them the truth as I do and let the best man win ?

WILLIAM

The trouble with you, my lad, is want of tact. You can handle stone, but you can't handle men. You must learn to humour fools if you want to get anything done.

JOHN

You stinking fox !

[JOHN *joins* HENRY, *and they go off muttering together, sinking their differences in their common grievance.*

GERVASE (*troubled*)

Master William, is it true, what they say ?

Listen to me, young man. At my age one learns that sometimes one has to damn one's soul for the sake of the work. Trust me, God shall have a choir fit for His service. Does anything else really matter?

[*He and* GERVASE *follow the others out.*

During the singing of the following Interlude, the scene-shifters set the stage to represent the site of the choir. The other three ANGELS *go up and stand above with* GABRIEL.

Every carpenter and workmaster that laboureth night and day, and they that give themselves to counterfeit imagery, and watch to finish a work;

The smith also sitting by the anvil, and considering the iron work, he setteth his mind to finish his work, and watcheth to polish it perfectly.

So doth the potter sitting at his work, and turning the wheel about with his feet, who is always carefully set at his work, and maketh all his work by number.

All these trust to their hands, and every one is wise in his work.

Without these cannot a city be inhabited, and they shall not dwell where they will nor go up and down;

They shall not be sought for in public council, nor sit high in the congregation;

But they will maintain the state of the world, and all their desire is in the work of their craft.

II

About two years have passed since the previous scene. WORKMEN
*go in and out, fetching tools and barrows from door, left, which
appears to lead to some kind of office or store-room, and carrying
out, right, blocks of dressed stone on hand-barrows, etc. About
half a dozen* LAY BROTHERS *and* WORKMEN *remain to work on
the stage. A general impression of bustle and movement is accen-
tuated by the entrance of a number of respectably dressed* PIL-
GRIMS, *chattering like jackdaws,—right.*

PILGRIMS (*they enter by twos and threes, gape vaguely about
and pass on and out by way of the steps*)
Beautiful, beautiful; and everything in such good taste.
. . . I wonder what it costs to keep the shrine going in
candles. . . . Two years they've been building now—
goodness knows how long it's going to take. . . . Dickon,
you bad boy, leave that saw alone. . . . Who did you say
the architect was ? Wilfrid somebody ? . . . My poor, dear
husband—such a sad sufferer—I was determined to make
the pilgrimage. . . . No doubt, it will be all very fine when
it's finished, but I don't think it's a patch on Lincoln. . . .
Shocking bad dinners they give you at the " Lamb "—
you'd better come and have a bite with us. . . . I beg your
pardon, madam, was that your foot ? Ah, the poor, dear,
martyred Archbishop ! Such a charming man. I saw him
when he came back from France—yes, really, he was as
close to me as I am to you. . . . Have you heard the one
about the three fat friars and the tinker's widow ? Well,
there were three begging friars. . . . So I said to her,

" Very well, you may take your wages and go." . . . It came to me as I was kneeling there that God would most surely have pity upon my sister. . . . I must say it comes out more expensive than I'd reckoned for. And I was abominably cheated that night we lay at Rochester. . . . The King must be a very naughty man to have killed the poor Archbishop. . . . There ! I told you it was only putting ideas into the child's head. . . . Bad business, that fire, and if you ask me, I don't believe the true story ever came out. . . . Yes, darling, ever so sorry—barefoot in a white sheet. . . . Indeed, I have a very great devotion to St. Thomas. . . . This Purbeck marble's all the rage, but I don't care about it myself . . . etc., etc.

[*They trail away, still chattering. During the confusion,* GERVASE *and* WILLIAM *have made their entrances, right,* GERVASE *crossing the stage and vanishing into doorway, left, while* WILLIAM *sits at a trestle-table, centre, and waits resignedly for his workshop to get clear. As the stage empties, the* ANGELS *come down again and take up their former positions.*

CASSIEL

Two years of toil are passed ; what shall I write
About this architect ?

MICHAEL

A schedule here,
Long as my sword, crammed full of deadly sins ;
Jugglings with truth, and gross lusts of the body,
Drink, drabbing, swearing ; slothfulness in prayer ;
With a devouring, insolent ambition
That challenges disaster.

CH

CASSIEL

These are debts;
What shall I set upon the credit side?

GABRIEL

Six columns, and their aisles, with covering vaults
From wall to arcading, and from thence again
To the centre, with the keystones locking them,
All well and truly laid without a fault.

CASSIEL

No sum of prayer to balance the account?

GABRIEL

Ask Raphael, for prayers are in his charge.

CASSIEL

Come, Raphael, speak; or is thy censer cold?
Canst thou indeed find any grace in William
The builder-up of Canterbury?

RAPHAEL

Yes.

[*He swings his censer, which gives out a cloud of incense.*

Behold, he prayeth; not with the lips alone,
But with the hand and with the cunning brain
Men worship the Eternal Architect.
So, when the mouth is dumb, the work shall speak
And save the workman. True as mason's rule
And line can make them, the shafted columns rise
Singing like music; and by day and night
The unsleeping arches with perpetual voice
Proclaim in Heaven, to labour is to pray.

MICHAEL

Glory to God, that made the Firmament !

[*Enter* GERVASE, *left.*

GERVASE

Here are the letters for you to sign, Master William. These to Caen, about the next shipment of stone; these to Dover, with instructions for the unloading and carriage. I have mentioned the matter of the damaged crane and told them it must be made good at their own expense.

[*Hands pen and inkhorn.*

WILLIAM

Thanks, Father Gervase.

[*Signs letters.*

GERVASE

This is the invoice for the oak roofing-beams. And there is an enclosure I can't quite understand. Something about the commission.

WILLIAM (*hastily*)

That has no business to be there. Idiots ! It refers to a private transaction. Give it to me. I will deal with it myself. Anything more ?

[*Taking paper and pocketing it.*

GERVASE

Do you mind looking at this consignment note ? We seem to be fifty scaffold-poles short; but I will have them checked again.

WILLIAM

Good. I can trust you to get it put in order. I don't know what we should have done these two years without your vigilant eye and skilful pen.

GERVASE

I wish I could do more to help. But my hands are no good for anything but writing. I should have loved to take a more active part in the work. (*Smiling.*) I must be content to be the man with only one talent, and make it go as far as I can.

[*Enter* HUBERT, *right.*

WILLIAM

If every one would make good use of his own talent and let others do the same, the world would move faster. Well, Brother Hubert, what's the trouble?

HUBERT

Well, sir, if you'd kindly take a look at this here last lot of lime (*presenting specimens of lime and mortar on a shovel*). If lime you can call it. What they've done to it I *don't* know, but it don't seem to have no body in it as you might say. It don't bind right. You should hear what my lads has to say about it.

WILLIAM

Yes. Poor slack stuff. Where did this come from?

GERVASE

From Jocelyn's. You remember, the Father Treasurer wanted the order given to them. He said Thomas Clay's price was excessive.

WILLIAM

I wish the Father Treasurer would allow me to know my own job. Tell him—no, don't tell him anything. Order in a fresh lot from Thomas Clay's as before, instructing him to charge it up at Jocelyn's price and send me a private note of the difference. We can adjust it on that timber account. Do you understand? If these timber merchants are knaves enough to offer me a five per cent commission for giving them the contract and Father Stephen is fool enough to grudge a few pounds extra for first-class material, all right. We play off the knave against the fool, get what we want, and save argument.

HUBERT

Ay, that's so. What the Father Treasurer don't see won't worry him.

GERVASE

But is it honest?

HUBERT

All I know is, this here lime ain't honest. Prior Wibert, him as built the Water-Tower, wouldn't never have asked his masons to put up with cheap rubbish like this here.

WILLIAM (*to* GERVASE)

No, of course it's not honest. And it's not exactly safe. That is, it's liable to misconstruction, if proclaimed upon the housetops. But the Lord commended the unjust steward.

HUBERT

You can't make bricks without straw, nor yet mortar without lime. And if Prior Wibert, rest his soul, was alive, he'd say the same.

WILLIAM

Cheer up, little churchman. Take thy bill and sit down quickly and write fifty. Nobody's robbing the Church.

[*Exit* GERVASE, *left, still a trifle unhappy about it.*

H'm. Unfortunate. He'll lie awake all night wrestling with his conscience, and probably let the whole thing out to the Father Treasurer. Can't be helped. Sufficient for the day. . . . How about the new arch? D'you think she's settled in? I'd like to get those supports out to-day.

HUBERT

Been over every inch of her, sir, and I think she'll do. We're getting the tackle up now.

WILLIAM

Let me know when you're ready; I don't want anything started till I come. What do you think of the plan for the roof and clerestory?

HUBERT

Grand, sir, grand. I only wish Prior Wibert, good man, was alive to see it. Always a man for new ideas, was Prior Wibert. Ah! He'd have loved that tall shafting and the way the cross-ribbing is made to carry the span. " Mark my words, Hubert," he used to say to me, " the arch is the secret of building. We ain't half learned yet," he'd say, " what the arch can carry when it's put to it."

WILLIAM

He was right, there. But we're finding out. We're finding out every day. Greece never guessed it; Rome only half understood it; but our sons will know in the years to come. (*With rising excitement.*) We all have our dreams, Hubert. Churches we shall never live to see. Arch shouldering arch, shaft, vault and keystone, window and arcading, higher and wider and lighter, lifting roof, tower, spire, into the vault of heaven—columns slender as lily-stalks—walls only a framework for the traceries— living fountains of stone——

HUBERT

That's so, Master, that's so. That's the way to build. Each stone carrying his neighbour's burden, as you might say.

WILLIAM

A triumph of balance, eh, Hubert ? A delicate adjustment of interlocking stresses. Look ! there was an idea came into my head last night.

[*He sketches on a block of stone.*
Enter STEPHEN *and* MARTIN, *right.*

STEPHEN

Well, I must say, it's rather inconsiderate. Still, we mustn't let the opportunity slip.

MARTIN

Certainly not; rich benefactors have to be humoured. Nobody knows that better than he does. Will you tackle him ?

STEPHEN

If you like. Er—Master William !

WILLIAM

What can I do for you, Father Treasurer ?

STEPHEN

Forgive me for interrupting you—I know you're very busy, but the fact is, we have a visitor——

MARTIN

Rather an important visitor.

STEPHEN

The Lady Ursula de Warbois——

[*Enter* THEODATUS, *right. He has his sleeves tucked up, and a coarse apron over his habit, and carries a trowel.*

MARTIN

We had been hoping she would come——

STEPHEN

She has just arrived and asked to see the Father Prior.

MARTIN

She is with him now. Father Theodatus, have you heard ? The Lady Ursula is with the Father Prior !

THEODATUS

Indeed ?

[*He goes across to speak to one of the* WORKMEN.

WILLIAM

Come, sirs. All this excitement is scarcely becoming to
your cloth. Is the lady young and beautiful? And what
is she doing with the Father Prior, or he with her?

[WORKMEN *snigger*.

THEODATUS

Master William! Pray control your tongue.

WILLIAM

There! you see you have shocked Father Theodatus.

STEPHEN

The Lady Ursula is the widow of an exceedingly wealthy
knight.

MARTIN

She has come to reside in Canterbury; and has several
times expressed interest in the work. To-day she has come
and wants to see over the new choir——

STEPHEN

If she is pleased with what she sees, she will probably
be good for a handsome subscription.

WILLIAM

Oh, very well. Take her where you like. Better stand clear
of the new arch, though. We're going to get the supports
out, and it might come down. You never know—eh,
Hubert?

HUBERT

That's right. You never know.

STEPHEN

Yes—but the point is, she particularly wants to meet the architect and be shown round personally.

MARTIN

She wants to see the plans, and have everything explained to her.

WILLIAM

T'cha ! women always want explanations. But they never listen, and wouldn't understand a word if they did. I've no use for women—not in working hours.

THEODATUS (*gloomily*)

The curse came by a woman.

WILLIAM

Well—if it comes to that, so did *you*, Father Theodatus.

HUBERT

That's right. Women are a curse—but we can't get *into* the world, nor *on* in the world without 'em.

MARTIN

Well, Master William, I'm sure you will oblige her. People always like to talk to the architect. The human touch, you know. It's always good publicity.

WILLIAM

Oh, very well, I suppose one must make one's self a martyr to publicity. Go and keep an eye on the lads, Hubert; I'll come as soon as I'm free.

[*Going,* STEPHEN *and* MARTIN *offer to accompany him.*
No, thanks. I can find my own way. Don't you run your

heads into temptation. *Sed libera nos a malo*—deliver us from the apple and all its consequences.

[*Exit, right, with* HUBERT.

STEPHEN

Dear me ! I hope he will behave with discretion.

MARTIN

Never fear. He can bridle his tongue when he likes. He is a politic man. Remember how he persuaded us into the expense of re-building.

STEPHEN

Yes—we have had some experience of his policy. Well— he wheedled money out of us; let him now wheedle it out of the Lady Ursula.

MARTIN

At any rate, he is a first-class workman. He gives us good value for our money.

STEPHEN

Does he ? I hope he does. Sometimes I have my doubts. From something one of the carriers let fall the other day, I am inclined to suspect him of—some irregularities.

MARTIN

Oh, surely not ! The accounts all go through your hands and the correspondence through those of Father Gervase.

STEPHEN

Father Gervase ? Do you think a crafty old fox like that hasn't the wit to hoodwink a young and innocent church-man like Father Gervase ? Is he in the office, by the way ?

63

I am inclined to give him a caution. (*Calling left.*) Father
Gervase !

GERVASE (*emerging, left, with letters*)

Yes, Father Stephen ?

STEPHEN

Tell me; since you have been handling Master William's
letters, have you ever had any reason to suspect any
financial irregularities ?

GERVASE (*taken aback*)

Financial irregularities ?

STEPHEN

Tampering with the estimates ? Fudging the accounts ?
Pocketing commissions and that sort of thing ? Doing little
deals on the side ?

GERVASE (*recovering himself; with confidence*)

I am quite positive, Father Stephen, that Master William
has never cheated the Church of a single penny, and never
would. He thinks of nothing, lives for nothing, but the
integrity of his work. If you knew him as well as I do,
working with him these two years, you would be sure of
that.

STEPHEN

I am glad to hear it. But keep your eyes open. I have
heard stories, and I am not altogether satisfied.

GERVASE

Would it not be better to speak openly to Master William
himself ?

THEODATUS

Of course it would; but they are afraid to. Why ? Because the man has managed to get the ear of the Father Prior—and because they don't want him to throw up the job in the middle—and because, having once put their hands to dirty tools, they don't know how to draw back. (*To* STEPHEN *and* MARTIN) No man can serve God and mammon. God's House should be built with prayer. You are trying to build it with worldly wisdom and worldly lucre. Look at all those pilgrims ! How many of them have clean hands and pure hearts ?

MARTIN

We cannot see into their hearts.

THEODATUS

Have you listened to their talk ? One in ten may be sincere. The rest are idle men and gadding women, making pilgrimage an excuse for a holiday trip—compounding for old sins by committing new ones. All they come for is to drink and gossip in alehouses, tell each other dirty stories, pick up loose companions, waste their own time and other people's, and gabble through a few perfunctory prayers at top speed, so as to have more time for sight-seeing.

GERVASE

Are you not a little uncharitable ?

STEPHEN

Most of them are very worthy people. And after all, we can't do without their money.

65

THEODATUS

If you had faith, you could. You degrade the Church by these vulgar and dubious methods of publicity.

MARTIN

Really, Father Theodatus ! This is monstrous. The Father Prior himself entrusted me with the publicity side of the appeal. I have taken great pains to get these pilgrimages properly advertised. And this is my reward !

GERVASE

Brethren ! brethren ! All the workmen are listening to you.
[*Enter* WILLIAM, *right, with* URSULA.

MARTIN

Let them listen !

THEODATUS

I do not care who hears me !

WILLIAM

Pray, madam, mind your head—the doorway is rather low. One step down. Allow me. This is just a little corner of our workshop, where—— Walter ! Hugh ! Simon ! Is nobody doing any work to-day ? Do you take it for the Feast of St. Lazybones ? (*The* WORKMEN *hurriedly return to their tasks.*) Walter—that corner is out of true. And here, you ! Is that the way to treat your tools ? . . . I beg your pardon, madam. The moment my back is turned, everything seems to come to a standstill.

URSULA

No wonder. Without the heart, how can the limbs do their office ? You are the heart of the undertaking.

WILLIAM (*formally*)

It is very good of you to say so. I think you know Father
Stephen, the Treasurer? Father Martin, the Guest-
Brother? Father Theodatus, the Sacristan? And Father
Gervase, who is Clerk and Historian to the Chapter,
and is good enough to deal with my correspondence in
his spare time. (*To* GERVASE) Have those letters gone?

GERVASE

I am just taking them to the messenger.
    [*Exit* GERVASE, *right.*

MARTIN

And what, madam, do you think of our Cathedral?

URSULA

I think it must be the most beautiful in the world. And
how glorious the new choir will be when it is finished!
Master William has described it all to me and has promised
to show me all his plans and drawings. That was a promise,
was it not, Master William?

WILLIAM

Certainly—if you are really interested.

URSULA

Of course I am interested. I am glad I have come to live
in Canterbury. It will be so exciting to watch the work
going on from day to day. A widow needs an interest in
life. And it will be a great comfort to live under the
protection of blessed St. Thomas.

67

MARTIN

Thousands of the suffering and bereaved have already found healing and consolation by his benign intervention. Only a few weeks ago, out of a large congregation of worshippers who attended a special service——

[*Bell begins to ring.* MONKS *enter, right, and file across the stage and down the steps.* WORKMEN *lay down their tools and go out, right, with dinner-baskets.*

THEODATUS

That is the bell for nones.

[*Exit down steps.*

MARTIN

I will tell you presently about the special service.

[*Exeunt* STEPHEN *and* MARTIN *down steps.*

WILLIAM

Do you propose to attend nones ? The lower part of the nave is available for the laity.

URSULA

No ; I propose to see those drawings of yours.

WILLIAM

I do not think you came here to see architectural drawings.

URSULA

I came—to see the architect. (*Pause.*) Did you realise that this was not the first time we had met ?

WILLIAM

I realised it perfectly. I had the honour to pick up your glove yesterday in the market-place.

URSULA

I was much indebted to you for the courtesy.

WILLIAM

I was much indebted to you for the opportunity. I am an opportunist. So, I fancy, are you. We have that much in common.

URSULA

Is that an impertinence, I wonder?

WILLIAM

Yes.

URSULA

I ought to be offended with you.

WILLIAM

If you are wise, you will be. Let us be plain.
The first time our eyes met, we knew one another
As fire knows tinder. You have seen what havoc
Fire works. Let be.

URSULA
I do not fear the fire.

WILLIAM

My fire should be a lamp to light the world,
Fed with my life, consuming only me;
Will you not learn that it is perilous
To play with fire? That it is death to come
Between the man and the work? In one man's life
Is room for one love and no more—one love;
I am in love with a dream.

Dн

URSULA

Tell me your dreams
Sitting by the fire, seeing pictures in the fire,
Visions and dreams.

WILLIAM

Your old men shall dream dreams
And your young men see visions—but not your women.
What use have women for the dreams of a man
Save to destroy them ? What does a woman know
Of the love of knowledge, passing the love of women ?
The passion of making, beside which love's little passion
Shows brittle as a bubble ?—To raise up beauty from ashes
Like the splendour of resurrection ; to see the stone
Knit unto stone and growing, as in the womb
Bone grows to bone ; to build a world out of nothing—
That is my dream ; that is the craftsman's dream,
The power and the glory, the kingdom of God and man—
Of man, never of woman. Women create
Passively, borne on a wind of lust, for a whim,
At the caprice of a man, in a smile, in a spasm
Of the flesh ; we, with the will, with the blood, with the
    brain,
All the desire of the soul, the intent of the mind.
Now do you understand what my dreams are
And why they are not for you ?

URSULA

I understand.
Knowledge and work—knowledge is given to man
And not to woman ; and the glory of work

70

To man and not to woman. But by whom
Came either work or knowledge into the world ?
Not by the man. God said, " Ye shall not know;
Knowledge is death." And Adam was afraid.
But Eve, careless of peril, careless of death,
Hearing the promise, " Ye shall be as gods,"
Seized knowledge for herself, and for the man,
And all the sons of men; knowledge, like God;
Power to create, like God; and, unlike God,
Courage to die. And the reward for her
Was sorrow; but for Adam the reward
Was work—of which he now contrives to boast
As his peculiar glory, and in one breath
Denies it to the woman and blames her for it,
Winning the toss both ways. My simple Adam,
It is too late to scare woman with risks
And perils—woman, that for one splendid risk
Changed the security of Paradise,
Broke up the loom and pattern of creation,
Let in man's dream on the world, and snatched the torch
Of knowledge from the jealous hand of God
So that the fire runs in man's blood for ever.

WILLIAM (*carried away*)

So that she runs like fire in a man's blood
For ever ! Take what thou wilt—the risk, the sorrow,
The fire, the dream—and in the dream's end, death.

GABRIEL

Thus Eve cast down the gauntlet in God's face:
" My will for Thine; man's purpose against God's ;

Slay me and slay the man, slay all my seed,
But let man's knowledge and man's work go on."

MICHAEL

Thus God took up the gauntlet in Eve's face.
Having, like man, courage to look on death:
" My Son for thy sons, and God's blood for man's;
Crucify God, but let the work go on."

CASSIEL

By man came sin.

RAPHAEL

   O felix culpa, quae
Talis et tanti meruit Redemptoris !

HUBERT (*off*)

Master William ! Master William !

WILLIAM

There ! that means work. You see what happens when one
starts this kind of thing. Go now. They are coming out
of church. Quickly—or we shall have Father Martin and
the special service all over again. I will come to your
lodging after supper.

URSULA (*on the steps*)

Bringing your dreams with you.
 [*Exit down steps. Enter* HUBERT, *right.*

HUBERT

Master ! The arch is ready when you are.

WILLIAM

I am coming. Work, Hubert, work. Sometimes one persuades one's self that it all means something to somebody.

HUBERT

Do you think the gracious lady will be moved to contribute to the building fund ?

WILLIAM

H'm. I had forgotten that aspect of the matter. Yes—I shouldn't be surprised if she did.

HUBERT

The blessed saints be praised for it.

WILLIAM

I wonder !

[*Exeunt* WILLIAM *and* HUBERT, *right.*

THE YOUNG CHERUB (*suddenly*)

Why did God create mankind in two different sorts, if it makes so much trouble ?

[*The* ANGELS *are inexpressibly shocked.*

RAPHAEL

Hush ! you musn't ask Why.

MICHAEL

Angels never ask Why.

GABRIEL

Only men ask Why.

CASSIEL

And you see what happened to them, just for asking Why.

MICHAEL

Do you want to eat of the Tree of Knowledge, like Adam and Eve?

GABRIEL

And find Michael there, with his big sword?

RAPHAEL

And put our Master to the trouble and pain of another crucifixion?

CASSIEL

Or start another war, like that lost brother whom we must not name?

ALL

Criticising God's creation! I never heard of such a thing!

CHOIR

Shall we that are but worms, but silk-worms, but glow-worms, chide God that He hath made slow-worms, and other venomous creeping things?

Shall we that are all discord, quarrel the harmony of His creation or His providence?

Can an apothecary make a sovereign treacle of vipers and other poisons, and cannot God admit offences and scandals into His physic?

As soon as he had made light (which was His first creature) He took pleasure in it; He said it was good; He was glad of it; glad of the sea, glad of the earth, glad of the sun, and moon, and stars, and He said of every one, It is good.

III

The scene is as before; two more years have passed; WALTER, HUGH *and* GEOFFREY, *lay workmen, are engaged in polishing marble rather up-stage.*

    [*Enter* SIMON, *right, and crosses to door, left.*

SIMON (sings)

  The animals went in two by two,
    Hey, ho, nonny !
  Said the dog, Bow-wow ! said the cat, Mew, mew !
    Spring is the time for love !

    [*Exit left.*

WALTER

Spring, indeed ! I wish the spring were here. It hasn't stopped raining for three months.

HUGH

More like four. We've had vile weather ever since the eclipse last September. What a climate !

WALTER

I knew that eclipse meant bad luck.

GEOFFREY

Well, it's not raining to-day.

HUGH

Bad luck ? If we never get worse luck than a bit of bad weather, I don't care how many eclipses we have.

WALTER

We ain't heard the last of the eclipse yet, mark my words.

HUGH

You and your prophecies ! What are you grumbling about ? Job's going well enough, ain't it ? Four years, and here we've finished the triforium and the clerestory, and the key of the great arch will be put in to-day. Not too bad, in four years.

[*Re-enter* SIMON, *left, trundling a coil of rope, wound on a drum.*

GEOFFREY

Ah ! he's a good worker, is Master William. And a fast worker. Knows what he's about. He's the sort of master I can do with. Strict, and drives you like the devil, but I don't mind that.

HUGH

That's right. I respect a master that's a good worker. When Master William works, he works.

WALTER

And when he plays (*with a meaning grin*), he plays ! Him and the Lady Ursula !

HUGH

Well, I don't mind that, either. That's their affair.

SIMON

Quite right, Hugh. The day for labour and the night for —sleep.

(*Sings*) Two by two they went into the ark,
>   *Hey, ho, nonny !*
> The doors were shut, they were all in the dark,
>   *Spring is the time for love !*

GEOFFREY
She's somewhere about the place now.

WALTER
Who is ? Lady Ursula ?

GEOFFREY
Yes. Takes a lot of interest. Always putting up a bit o' prayer, or coming to see how the job's getting on, or calling on the Father Treasurer with a little donation to something.

SIMON (*sings*)
> But when old Noah opened the door,
>   *Hey, ho, nonny !*
> They all came out by three and four,
>   *Spring is the time for love !*

[*Enter* PRIOR *and* THEODATUS, *right.*

HUGH
It's a wonder the good fathers don't see through it.

GEOFFREY
Maybe they do. Maybe it pays them to wink t'other eye. Lady Ursula's rich. It don't do to offend rich folks.

THEODATUS
You hear that, Father Prior ?

WALTER

All the same, mark my words, no good will come of it.
That eclipse wasn't sent for nothing.

HUGH

Ah, come off it. You and your eclipse !

SIMON (*sings*)

Who d'ye think had been playing tricks ?
Hey, ho, nonny !
They went in two and they came out six,
Spring is the time for love !

THEODATUS

For shame, my son, for shame ! We cannot have these
lewd songs here.

[*He comes down past* SIMON *to the steps, with the* PRIOR.

SIMON

Sorry, Father.

[*He goes out, left.*

THEODATUS

So it goes on, Father, day after day—
Songs in the workshop, sniggering in the dortor,
Unbecoming gossip among the novices,
Heads wagged in the market-place, and tales going round
In the ale-house, fingers pointed everywhere
At William of Sens, the Cathedral architect—
A notorious evil liver, a seducer of women,
A taker of bribes——

PRIOR (*mildly*)

That was not proved, I fancy.

THEODATUS

A cunning liar, that boasts of pulling the wool
Over the eyes of the fat, innocent monks;
A man without truth, without shame. It is not respectable;
It is not right.

PRIOR

You must not say, without truth,
Lest you should hear the very stones cry out
Against you. Truth is glorious; but there is one
Glory of the sun, another of the moon,
And all the truth of the craftsman is in his craft.
Where there is truth, there is God; and where there is
glory,
There is God's glory too.

THEODATUS (*sullenly*)

Craft is the word.
We could do better without William's craft
In more ways than in one. I would rather have
A worse-built church with a more virtuous builder.

PRIOR

Make God the loser for your conscience' sake?
This is God's House, and if on any pretext
We give him less than the best, we shall cheat God
As William never cheated God, nor us.
He that bestowed the skill and the desire

79

To do great work is surely glad to see
That skill used in His service.

Skill is not all.
The kingdom of Heaven is won by righteousness,
Not skill. He cannot wish His work performed
Save with clean hands and a pure heart.

PRIOR

My son,
Will you not let God manage His own business?
He was a carpenter, and knows His trade
Better, perhaps, than we do, having had
Some centuries of experience; nor will He,
Like a bad workman, blame the tools wherewith
He builds His City of Zion here on earth.
For God founded His Church, not upon John,
The loved disciple, that lay so close to His heart
And knew His mind—not upon John, but Peter;
Peter the liar, Peter the coward, Peter
The rock, the common man. John was all gold,
And gold is rare; the work might wait while God
Ransacked the corners of the earth to find
Another John; but Peter is the stone
Whereof the world is made. So stands the Church,
Stone upon stone, and Christ the corner-stone
Carved of the same stuff, common flesh and blood,
With you, and me, and Peter; and He can,
Being the alchemist's stone, the stone of Solomon,

Turn stone to gold, and purge the gold itself
From dross, till all is gold.

THEODATUS

    To purge—to burn !
He makes His ministers a flaming fire—
And are not we His ministers ? Shall not we
Lay axe to the rotten root, trunk, branch ? destroy,
Make bonfire of this scandal in the Church
And burn God's honour clean ?

PRIOR

     God is a man,
And can defend His honour, being full-grown
In wisdom and in stature. We need not
Play nursemaid to the Babe of Bethlehem
To shield Him from the harlot and the thief,
Or keep those tender, innocent hands from harm
That bear the sharp nails' imprint, and uphold
The axis of the spheres. He can touch dirt
Without defilement, for Himself hath said,
" What I have cleansed, that call not thou unclean."

THEODATUS

But while His laws are broken in our sight
Must we stand by, and smile, and still do nothing ?

PRIOR

Do your own work, while yet the daylight lasts.
Look that it be well done; look not beyond it.
I charge you, on your holy obedience,

Set charity as a bridle on your tongue;
Talk not of William's nor another's faults,
Unless to God, Who hears but spreads no scandal.
Of this be sure: who will not have the Gospel
Shall have the Law; but in God's time, not ours.

[*Enter* SIMON *by door, left, carrying a small windlass.*

SIMON (*bursting irrepressibly into song*)
Every bird had found her mate,
Hey, ho, nonny !
They all came out by seven and eight,
Spring is the time for love !

[*He sets the windlass down, centre. Enter* WILLIAM, *right.*

WILLIAM

You are merry, Simon. Is that the rope to rig the travelling cradle ?

SIMON

Yes, sir.

WILLIAM

See that every inch of it is well tested before I go up. I'm not as young or as light as I was. Good morning, Father Prior. Ah ! Father Theodatus, you are just the man I was looking for. Pray will you help Simon to test that rope ? It is to hoist me up to the top of the great arch, and I have a value for my neck.

THEODATUS

Oh, by all means.

[*Moving up, left.*

WILLIAM

Simon is a good lad enough, but I would rather trust your vigilance. Young men's minds are apt to run astray.

[*During the following dialogue,* THEODATUS *takes the free end of the rope and begins to wind it off on to the windlass.* SIMON *stands by the drum, so that, as the rope is slowly wound off, they can both examine it for flaws. They occupy the stage from centre to left.*]

PRIOR

Young men are not alone in that, Master William. The talk of the town comes to our ears sometimes, dull-witted old churchmen though we be. It seems that even a master architect may find interests outside his work.

WILLIAM

Outside his working *hours*, Father Prior.

PRIOR

I quite appreciate that. My dear son, as your father in God I might find many things to say to you. . . .

WILLIAM

But as a man of the world you doubt whether I should listen. It is a rare virtue to refrain even from good words.

PRIOR

Then I will speak only as a man of the world and urge the value of discretion.

WILLIAM

Father Theodatus would say, of hypocrisy.

PRIOR

Father Theodatus is not your employer. The Church is your employer, and it is my duty to speak for the Church.

WILLIAM

Very well. As my *employer*, to use your own blunt term, what fault have you to find with my private amusements ?

PRIOR

This; that instead of attending to their work, your workmen waste their time in gossip and backbiting about you. If you choose to be damned, you must; if you prefer to make a death-bed repentance, you may; but if an idle workman does an unsound job now, no repentance of yours will prevent it from bringing down the church some day or other.

WILLIAM *(after a pause)*

You are quite right. I congratulate you. You have found the one argument to which I am bound to listen. Were you a diplomat before you were a churchman ?

PRIOR

Perhaps.

[*Exit, right.*

WILLIAM *(looking after him)*

Or a soldier. The old man's a hard hitter and knows where to plant his blows. *(He goes up, back, to overlook the work of* WALTER *and* GEOFFREY, *speaking to* THEODATUS *and* SIMON *as he goes)* : Test it with the eye and the hand— don't trust to either alone.

MICHAEL

Are there no fires in Heaven, that every man
With his own hand, upon the anvil of sin
Forges the sword of judgment ? Gabriel, Raphael,
There is a sword in the making; look you to it.

[RAPHAEL *goes up and stands near* THEODATUS, *centre, and* GABRIEL *near* SIMON, *left.*

℣. The eyes of the Lord are in every place, beholding the evil and the good.

℟. Shall we continue in sin that grace may abound ? God forbid.

℣. He maketh His sun to rise on the evil and on the good;

℟. And sendeth rain upon the just and unjust.

[*Enter* URSULA, *right.*

URSULA

William !

WILLIAM (*turning quickly and coming to meet her*)
Ah ! You have come at a very good moment.

[*He leads her forward to the steps.*

SIMON (*watching them with interest*)
Oho ! look at that !

WILLIAM

We are just about to put in the key of the great arch.

THEODATUS

Turn away mine eyes from beholding vanity !

WILLIAM

If you will stand here presently and watch, you will see

Eh

me fly up to the top of the scaffold in a machine of my own devising—and down again, like blessed St. Paul in a basket !

THEODATUS (*hastily reciting with averted eyes*)
Sancta Maria, ora pro nobis;
Sancta Dei genetrix, ora pro nobis;
Sancta Virgo virginum, ora pro nobis.

[RAPHAEL *sets his censer gently swinging.*

URSULA
How amusing ! I hope it is safe.

SIMON (*over his shoulder to* GEOFFREY)
More headaches for Father Martin ! He don't like these goings-on. Says they look bad, and shock influential patrons.

WILLIAM
Never fear for that. But, hark'ee—we're in disgrace with the Prior.

THEODATUS
Mater castissima, ora pro nobis;
Mater inviolata, ora pro nobis;
Mater intemerata, ora pro nobis.

URSULA
Oh ! I ought not to have come.

WILLIAM
That was my fault. I asked you. I wanted you here.

GABRIEL
Take care, Simon ! There is a flaw in the rope.

[SIMON, *with his eyes on* WILLIAM *and* URSULA, *pays no attention.*

SIMON (*sings*)

The cat, the rat, the sow, the hen,
   Hey, ho, nonny !
They all came out by nine and ten,
   Spring is the time for love !

[*The rope runs through his heedless fingers.* GABRIEL *makes a despairing gesture, and looks across at* RAPHAEL. *The scandalised* THEODATUS *continues to pray with his eyes tight shut.*

THEODATUS

Virgo veneranda, ora pro nobis;
Virgo praedicanda, ora pro nobis;
Virgo potens, ora pro nobis.

URSULA

What does the Prior complain of? Scandal in the Cathedral ?

WILLIAM

Something like that.

THEODATUS

Vas honorabile, ora pro nobis;
Vas insigne devotionis, ora pro nobis;
Rosa mystica, ora pro nobis.

RAPHAEL

Take care, Theodatus ! There is a flaw in the rope.

THEODATUS

Turris Davidica, ora pro nobis;
Turris eburnea, ora pro nobis;
Domus aurea, ora pro nobis.

[RAPHAEL *flings away the censer, which rolls clanging down the steps. The rope, flaw and all, is wound off.*

URSULA

At least he cannot say that you think more of me than of your work.

WILLIAM

No, he has not said that.

THEODATUS

Agnus Dei, qui tollis peccata mundi, parce nobis Domine;
Agnus Dei, qui tollis peccata mundi, exaudi nos, Domine;
Agnus Dei, qui tollis peccata mundi, miserere nobis.

[*The rope is now all wound off.*

URSULA

He will not take the work away from you?

WILLIAM

He is too shrewd for that. Besides, God would not let him; He has put me here and will keep me here, Prior or no Prior.

WORKMAN (*putting his head in at the door, below*)

Master Hubert says, is that rope ready?

SIMON

Here you are, mate.

[*He picks up the windlass and takes it down to* WORKMAN, *who carries it out.*

URSULA

Do we presume too much upon God's mercy?

WILLIAM

We are the master-craftsmen, God and I—
We understand one another. None, as I can,
Can creep under the ribs of God, and feel
His heart beat through those Six Days of Creation;
Enormous days of slowly turning lights
Streaking the yet unseasoned firmament;
Giant days, Titan days, yet all too short
To hold the joy of making. God caught His breath
To see the poles of the world stand up through chaos;
And when He sent it forth, the great winds blew,
Carrying the clouds. And then He made the trees
For winds to rustle through—oak, poplar, cedar,
Hawthorn and elm, each with its separate motion—
And with His delicate fingers painted the flowers,
Numberless—numberless ! why make so many
But that He loved the work, as I love mine,
And saw that it was good, as I see mine ?—
The supple, swift mechanics of the serpent,
The beautiful, furred beasts, and curious fish
With golden eyes and quaintly-laced thin bones,
And whales like mountains loud with spurting springs,
Dragons and monsters in strange shapes, to make
His angels laugh with Him; when He saw those
God sang for joy, and formed the birds to sing.
And lastly, since all Heaven was not enough
To share that triumph, He made His masterpiece,
Man, that like God can call beauty from dust,
Order from chaos, and create new worlds

To praise their maker. Oh, but in making man
God over-reached Himself and gave away
His Godhead. He must now depend on man
For what man's brain, creative and divine
Can give Him. Man stands equal with Him now,
Partner and rival. Say God needs a church,
As here in Canterbury—and say He calls together
By miracle stone, wood and metal, builds
A church of sorts; *my* church He cannot make—
Another, but not that. This church is mine
And none but I, not even God, can build it.
Me hath He made vice-gerent of Himself,
And were I lost, something unique were lost
Irreparably; my heart, my blood, my brain
Are in the stone; God's crown of matchless works
Is not complete without my stone, my jewel,
Creation's nonpareil.

URSULA

    Hush ! God will hear you—
The priests say He is jealous. Tempt Him not
Lest He should smite and slay.

WILLIAM

      He will not dare;
He knows that I am indispensable
To His work here; and for the work's sake, He,
Cherishing, as good masons do, His tools,
Will keep me safe. When the last stone is laid
Then may He use me as He will; I care not;

The work is all; when that is done, good night—
My life till then is paramount with God.

URSULA

You make me shake to hear you. Blasphemy ! blasphemy !

WILLIAM

Sound sense. Fear nothing. I must leave you now;
The work waits for me, and that must not be;
Idleness is the only sin. Like God
I must be doing in my little world,
Lest, lacking me, the moon and stars should fail.

[*He goes out down the steps.*

URSULA (*watching him go*)

I am afraid; have mercy on him, Christ !

CASSIEL

Draw thy sword, Michael; the hour is come.

[MICHAEL *follows* WILLIAM *out, with his sword drawn in his hand.*

℣. Except the Lord build the house, their labour is but lost that build it.

℟. Except the Lord keep the city, the watchman waketh but in vain.

℣. The zeal of thine house hath eaten me up; and rebukes are fallen upon me.

℟. For Thou art great and doest wondrous things; Thou art God alone.

[*During the singing of these versicles, the three remaining* ANGELS *stand side by side at the top of the steps, with* URSULA *below them. Now they go up and stand on the plinth at the back of the stage,* RAPHAEL *and* GABRIEL *to right and left, with* CASSIEL *centre.*

CHOIR

The Lord is known to execute judgment; the ungodly is trapped in the work of his own hands.

For he hath said in his heart, Tush, I shall never be cast down; there shall no harm happen unto me.

The snares of death compassed me round about, and the pains of hell gat hold upon me.

I shall find trouble and heaviness, and I will call upon the name of the Lord: O Lord, I beseech Thee, deliver my soul.

[*The stage gradually fills with* MONKS *and* WORKMEN; *among them is a* YOUNG BOY.

MONKS AND WORKMEN

This is a brave day . . . the great arch finished . . . See, they are making ready to drop in the keystone . . . It is wonderful how well Master William's machines work— they have halved the labour of building . . . there's old Hubert—he'll be a proud man to-day . . . Laus Deo ! our new choir will be ready for us within the year . . . There it goes ! No, they're waiting for something . . . They're waiting for the architect . . . There he is, slung half-way up in the travelling cradle . . . Can't you see ? Come on, lad, up on my shoulder . . . There's the keystone slung aloft on the crane . . . Hurray ! Master William's up now —just getting to the top of the scaffolding . . . Get ready to cheer, boys. . . .

THE YOUNG BOY (*from his perch on the workman's shoulder, shrilly*)

Oh, look ! look at the angel—the terrible angel !

ALL

What's that ? An angel ? What ? Where ? Nonsense !

THE YOUNG BOY

High on the scaffold, with the drawn sword in his hand !

URSULA

Mother of God !

[*She falls upon the steps.*

A shout from the stage is succeeded by a heavy crash without from the far end of the building. Men run in, right.

ALL

He's fallen . . . Master William's down . . . He's killed . . . fifty feet at least . . . His foot slipped . . . No, the rope broke . . . What's happened ? . . . God have mercy on us ! . . . Run for help ! . . . Blessed Mary, pray for us ! . . Send for the Prior . . . Fetch a chirurgeon . . . The devil is abroad . . . No, it was an angel . . . Where's that boy who saw the angel ? . . . Here, the lady's fainted—give us a hand here to carry her in . . . Come along, let's see what's happened . . .

[*There is a general rush down the steps.*

URSULA (*to the men who are supporting her*)

Take me with you. (*But she is unable to stand.*) No—leave me ! Run and bring me word.

[*They leave her crouched on the steps and run out. The three* ANGELS *come down and follow the crowd out. Nobody is left but* THEODATUS, SIMON *and* URSULA.

SIMON

The rope ! God forgive me—I was talking and laughing. Father Theodatus, what have we done ?

THEODATUS

The rope ! God is avenged. But I did not mean—I did not think—if it had not been for your lewd songs and his own behaviour with this woman——

URSULA

Could You not break me and not him, O God ?

SIMON

We have killed him among us.

CHOIR

Out of the deep have I called unto Thee. O Lord, hear my voice.
O let Thine ears consider well the voice of my complaint.
If Thou, Lord, wilt be extreme to mark what is done amiss, O Lord, who may abide it ?
For there is mercy with Thee, therefore shalt thou be feared.
I look for the Lord, my soul doth wait for Him, in His word is my trust.
My soul fleeth unto the Lord; before the morning watch, I say, before the morning watch.

O Israel, trust in the Lord, for with the Lord there is
mercy, and with Him is plenteous redemption;
And He shall redeem Israel from all his sins.

[*During the singing of the psalm, the* PRIOR *has re-entered
from the lower end, with* HUBERT, GERVASE *and the* YOUNG
BOY. *They mount the steps.*

URSULA

Father ! Father ! In pity, tell me—is he dead ?

PRIOR

No, my poor child. But sorely maimed.

HUBERT

He will never be the same man again.

URSULA

Let me go to him.

PRIOR

Presently. The leech is with him now, seeing to his hurts.
Trust me, you shall see him presently. (*He goes on up steps
and sits, right.*) Now, Hubert, I must know how all this
came to pass.

HUBERT

My Lord Prior, there is no doubt at all. There was a flaw
in the rope. Just as the cradle came up to the level of the
scaffolding, bearing Master William, I saw with my eyes
the strands spring asunder. I stretched out my hands to
catch him, but I could not reach. If I could have done
anything—anything ! I would gladly have given my life.

GERVASE

So would I, Hubert.

Prior

I am sure you would.

Hubert

Such a craftsman ! such a craftsman ! So kind a master !
Just, zealous, generous—no fault in him at all.

Gervase

So faithful a servant of the Church ! Who will finish his
work now ? . . . He was my friend, too.

Hubert

What I should like to know is—who had the testing o' that
there rope ?

Simon (*flinging himself at the* Prior's *feet*)

It was I—it was my neglect. I have no excuse. I shall
never forgive myself.

Ursula

It was my fault. I was talking to William—distracting the
attention of them all. This is a judgment for our sin—his
and mine.

Theodatus

True; it was a judgment. Ask this boy here. Did he not
see the angel thrust him down ?

Prior

Yes, child. What is this about an angel ?

The Young Boy

It is true. I saw a great angel stand between heaven and
earth—all in gold and scarlet, with a drawn sword. Oh,

and he had great wings, too. He cut the rope and the cradle fell.

THEODATUS

There, you see ! it was a divine judgment.

HUBERT

Divine judgment ! The boy's dreaming. It was rank carelessness. Simon—who was at the other end of the rope when you tested it ? (SIMON *looks round at* THEODATUS, *waiting for him to speak*.) Speak up, man ! Who was it ?

PRIOR

I was there, Theodatus.

THEODATUS

Well, it was I. But I had nothing to do with it. You heard what the child said. It was a miracle.

PRIOR

I think we sometimes make disasters, and then call them miraculous judgments. Did you at any moment take hand or eye from the rope while you were testing it ?

THEODATUS

I cannot remember. (*Under the* PRIOR's *eye, he abandons this line of defence*.) *She* was there with William. For my soul's sake I could not look at them. I was saying my prayers . . .

HUBERT

Sayin' your prayers ! With the master's safety depending on you !

97

THEODATUS

God Himself laid the seal upon my eyes. I was His
appointed instrument to overthrow the wicked man.

PRIOR

Think what you say, my son. It is not for us
To ordain ourselves the ministers of vengeance;
For it must needs be that offences come,
But woe unto that man by whom the offence
Cometh; 'twere better he had not been born.
This is thy sin: thou hast betrayed the work;
Thou hast betrayed the Church; thou hast betrayed
Christ, in the person of His fellow-man.
What was the prayer wherein thou offer'dst up
Thy brother's life?

THEODATUS

The Litany of the Virgin.

PRIOR

Go to the church; repeat it once again,
Saying at every line: " This was the spear
With which I pierced the body of the Lord,"
Then come to me and ask for absolution.

THEODATUS

I will obey.

[*Exit* THEODATUS, *right.*

PRIOR

For you, my son and daughter,
You see how sin brings its own suffering;
Do not despair; God's mercy is very great. (*He rises.*)

Thou that hast visions of angels, come with me.
I am an old man. Let me have thy shoulder.
So. Thou shalt tell me more about the angel.

[*Exeunt* PRIOR *and* YOUNG BOY, *right.*

GERVASE (*helping* URSULA *to her feet*)
Madam, pray do not weep so. He would be sorry to see it.
I loved him, too. Let us go together to visit him.

URSULA

And supposing he can never work again ? What comfort
in this world for him ? And what forgiveness for any of us ?

[*Exeunt* GERVASE *and* URSULA, *right.*

HUBERT

Well, Simon, you've made a nice mess of it. There, there,
lad, I can see you're sorry. Don't 'ee lose heart, now. It's
a bad business, but we must make the best of it.

SIMON
Oh, Hubert !

[*Exeunt* HUBERT *and* SIMON, *right.*

During the singing of the following hymn, the ANGELS *return
and take up their places as at the beginning of the play.*

CHOIR
Plebs angelica
phalanx et archangelica
principans turma, virtus
Uranica,
ac potestas
almiphona.

Dominantia
numina divinaque
subsellia, Cherubim
aetherea
ac Seraphim
ignicoma,

Vos, O Michael
caeli satrapa,
Gabrielque vera
dans verba nuntia,

Atque Raphael,
vitae vernula,
transferte nos inter
Paradisicolas.

IV

Six months have passed since the preceding scene. During the singing of the interlude, GERVASE, *assisted by a* LAY-BROTHER, *is making up a couch in the centre of the stage. Enter, right,* MARTIN, *carrying a couple of large sheepskins.*

MARTIN

They told me you wanted some extra coverings for Master William's bed.

GERVASE

Thank you, brother. Why, this is very kind ! Surely these are the best fleeces.

MARTIN

They are usually kept for distinguished visitors. But Father Wulfram specially asked that you should have them. They will make Master William warm and comfortable—since he has taken this fancy for lying here.

GERVASE

We are in hopes he may sleep better close to his work. He is so restless. Day and night he thinks of nothing but the building, and frets to lie helpless and so far away. From here he can see the sun shine on the arches he has raised ; and when he lies wakeful in the early dawn it will comfort him to hear the clink of the mason's trowel and the carver's hammer heralding in the day.

[*The* LAY-BROTHER *sets a stool near the head of the couch, down-stage, and goes out, right.*

FH

MARTIN

Poor soul ! Well, let us praise God for this warm and seasonable weather. Now that the summer is come, he will take no hurt from his change of lodging.

[*The* LAY-BROTHER *returns with a jug of water, a horn drinking-vessel, and a candlestick, which he places on the stool.*

GERVASE

May it refresh him, soul and body ! But I fear he undertakes more than his strength will bear. He has insisted to-day on being carried to view the progress of the roof over the Choir and Crosses. It is impossible to move him without causing severe pain—and then he gives orders and excites himself. Indeed, it is too much for him.

MARTIN (*with some hesitation*)

I suppose nothing would induce him to resign the appointment ?

GERVASE

Part him from his work ? Oh, no ! It would be more bitter to him than death. And where should we get another like him ?

[*Exit* LAY-BROTHER, *right.*

MARTIN

Well, I don't know. It is true he has done magnificent work. But frankly, dear brother, a sick man with a crippled spine cannot have his eyes here, there and everywhere, and during this half-year since his accident things have not gone quite so well.

GERVASE

You know why that is. Some of the brethren do not work so loyally for Brother Hubert as they did for him.

MARTIN

Isn't that natural ? Hubert is an excellent craftsman, but, after all, he is only an oblate, and a man of no education. Now if Master William had appointed, let us say, Father Hilary——

GERVASE

Father Hilary does fine carving very prettily, but he's quite out of his depth when it comes to the practical side of building. Now, Brother Hubert understands his job inside out.

MARTIN

Of course, but—— Well, there you are ! You can't deny that there has been a certain amount of ill-feeling.

GERVASE (*bitterly*)

Jealousy, vanity, hatred, malice and all uncharitableness ! And these are churchmen, vowed to holy obedience and humility.

MARTIN

Beati pauperes spiritu. Beati mites.

GERVASE

Amen ! (*He examines the couch critically and gives a punch to the pillows. Re-enter* LAY-BROTHER, *right, with a crucifix in his hand and a large bundle of papers under his arm.*) Ah, thanks, Brother Robert. (*He sets the crucifix on the stool with the other things.*) Better put the papers on that other stool for the

moment. (LAY-BROTHER *puts them on stool, right.*) There !
I think that is the best we can do.

[*Voices and footsteps off, right.*

MARTIN

I think they are bringing our patient in now.

GERVASE

I hope he is not too much exhausted.

[*Enter, right,* WILLIAM, *carried by* THEODATUS *and* SIMON.

WILLIAM

Ugh ! ugh ! Gently, you fools, gently. Do you want to
kill me ? You've had one good shot at it. Jolt, jolt, like
a couple of pack-asses. Clumsy idiots.

[*They lay him on the couch, to a running accompaniment of
groans and curses.*

THEODATUS

I am sorry. Did I hurt you ?

WILLIAM

Oh, no ! Only jarred me to pieces, that's all.

GERVASE (*arranging pillows*)

Is that a little easier ? I'm afraid you have over-tired
yourself. Are you in great pain ?

WILLIAM

Oh, I daresay it'll be worse in Purgatory.

MARTIN (*pouring out water*)

You have been out too long in the hot sun.

WILLIAM (*drinking*)

Thanks. Sorry, Simon. Don't mind me, Father Theodatus. It's only bad temper. The Prior set you a hard penance when he appointed you beast of burden to a sick man.

[*Exit* LAY-BROTHER.

THEODATUS

No, indeed. There is nothing I would more gladly do. I deserve far more than that for the evil I did you.

WILLIAM

Oh, stop blaming yourself. What's done can't be helped. Blame God, or the devil, or whoever looks after these things. Where's Hubert? I want him here. Go and fetch Brother Hubert, for God's sake, somebody. (*Exeunt* SIMON *and* THEODATUS, *right.*) Why haven't my papers been brought down?

GERVASE (*bringing stool with papers and setting it by the couch up-stage*)

They are all here. I will put them handy for you.

MARTIN

Will you not rest a little first?

WILLIAM

No, I will not. Leave me alone, can't you? Gervase, find me the measurements for those corbels. They've got them all wrong, as I knew they would. (*Enter* HUBERT, *right.*) Just because I'm not there to stand over them all the time—— Oh, Hubert, come and look at this. What did I tell you ? I knew it was not my measurements that were wrong. Can't you remember anything you're told ?

HUBERT

I am sure, sir, I gave Father Hilary the measurements exactly as you gave them to me. But he would have it as his own way was the right one, and he told the men under him——

WILLIAM

Father Hilary ! Why should they pay any attention to Father Hilary ? If I had the use of my limbs I'd give them something to remind them who's in charge here. But I have to lie helpless as a log while you make a mess of it among you. Never mind. Not your fault. Gervase, give me pen and ink—I'll show you how you can put it right. (GERVASE *fetches pen and ink from bench, left.*) Lift me up, somebody. (MARTIN *lifts him up.*) Ugh ! Now, see here . . . I've got an idea about this. . . .

[*He begins to draw on the plan, but is overcome by faintness.*

HUBERT

Dear master, leave it until to-morrow.

WILLIAM

It looks as though I shall have to. All right, Hubert. Don't worry. We'll put it straight in the morning. (GER-VASE *and* MARTIN *take away the drawing materials and settle him back on his pillows.*) Oh, God ! Shall I never be able to do anything again ?

[*Enter* LAY-BROTHER, *right, with a bowl of soup and a trencher of bread.*

MARTIN (*soothingly*)

You work too hard. You have over-tired yourself. You will feel better when you have eaten. (GERVASE *takes the bowl and hands it to* WILLIAM, *and the* LAY-BROTHER *goes out.*) Come away now, Brother Hubert. He must be persuaded to rest. (*He bustles* HUBERT *away, right, then turns at the door as* ERNULPHUS *and* PAUL *pop their heads round it.*) Here are some visitors for you.

[*Enter* PAUL, *carrying a bunch of roses and something done up in a cabbage-leaf, and* ERNULPHUS, *obviously concealing some offering under his habit. Exeunt* MARTIN *and* HUBERT.

ERNULPHUS

May we come in ? Pax tecum, my son, pax tecum.

WILLIAM (*in a dispirited growl*)

Et cum spiritu tuo.

ERNULPHUS

And how do you feel this evening ?

WILLIAM (*with a wry face, but not unkindly*)

Horrible !

ERNULPHUS

T—t—t—t—t !

PAUL

It's this dreadful hot weather. Very trying. I don't know when I remember such a trying June. I'm sure we never had such unwholesome heat when I was a boy. I was nearly melted away, working in the garden. And the greenfly gets worse every year. There never was such a year for greenfly. Everything smothered. Still, I've

107

managed to find a few roses (*presenting them*), and see !
A dozen or so of the early strawberries. I thought you
might like them for your supper.

WILLIAM (*genuinely touched*)

That's very good of you, Father Paul. Are they the first ?

PAUL

The very first. Nobody else has had any—not even the
Father Prior. I hope you will find them sweet. Though I
must say, fruit doesn't seem to have the flavour it had in
my young days. Still, such as they are, there they are.

[*He puts them on the stool, down-stage.*

WILLIAM

I shall enjoy them immensely. I don't know anything
more refreshing than early strawberries.

ERNULPHUS

Oho ! don't you ? I do. (*He produces a stout little flask from
under his habit.*) Just you try this. A reviving cordial water
from our own distillery. Not too fiery, and full of healthful
properties. Made from herbs, according to our special
recipe.

[*Puts it on the stool.*

WILLIAM

Thank you ; thank you very much. I will drink it to the
healths of both of you.

PAUL

Oh, but it is your own health we must all wish and pray
for. We do pray for you, of course. Night and morning.
And remember you at Mass. Eh, Father Ernulphus ?

ERNULPHUS

Always. All of us. So you mustn't lose heart. Oh, dear, no. Now we had better run away, or we shall tire you out. Good night, my son. May God watch over and restore you !

PAUL

Our Lady and all the blessed saints have you in their keeping.

[PAUL *and* ERNULPHUS *trundle amiably off, right.*

WILLIAM

Good old souls ! This is what I have come to, Gervase—to be nursed and coddled, and comforted like a child with strawberries. Ah, well. You can tuck me up for the night and leave me to my own hobgoblins.

GERVASE (*taking the supper things away and helping him to lie down*)

To the holy Angels, rather. There ! is that comfortable ?

WILLIAM

Yes, thank you, my boy.

GERVASE (*with a little assumption of authority*)

Do not forget your prayers.

WILLIAM

Very well, Father.

GERVASE

Benedicat te omnipotens Deus, Pater, et Filius et Spiritus Sanctus. Amen.

WILLIAM

Amen.

GERVASE (*going out, right*)

Sleep in peace. Hubert and I will be at hand if you should need anything.

[*Exit, left.*

WILLIAM *pulls out a rosary, mechanically counts the first decade, then tosses it away impatiently.*

CHOIR

O lux beata trinitas,
Et principalis unitas,
Jam sol recedit igneus;
Infunde lumen cordibus.

RAPHAEL

Michael.

GABRIEL

Michael.

CASSIEL

Michael, thou watchman of the Lord ! What of the night ?
Watchman, what of the night ?

MICHAEL

The morning cometh, and also the night; if ye will enquire, enquire ye: return, come.

CHOIR

Te mane laudum carmine,
Te deprecamur vesperi,
Te nostra supplex gloria
Per cuncta laudet saecula.

[*Enter* THEODATUS, *right.*

THEODATUS

Master William, there is one without would speak with you.

WILLIAM

Who ?

THEODATUS

The Lady Ursula.

WILLIAM

What is the use of this ? I will not see her. It is always the same story. She asks to be my wife, my nurse, my servant —Heaven knows what; to devote her life, make reparation and all the rest of it. She shall not do it. I will not have people sacrificing themselves for me. It is monstrous. It is impossible. Tell her so.

THEODATUS

She says she is here for the last time. She is very unhappy. I think you ought—I beseech you to let her come.

WILLIAM

That is a new tune for you to sing, Father Theodatus.

THEODATUS

I have learnt a little charity of late. Let me beg of you.

WILLIAM

Oh, very well.

[THEODATUS *beckons in* URSULA *and goes out, right.*

URSULA

William, I have come to say good-bye. I will not trouble you any more. Since I am nothing to you now, and the world without you is nothing to me, I can but take refuge at the Throne of Grace and pray for both of us.

WILLIAM

That is folly, my dear. You, in a convent of nuns ! Go and be happy, and forget me.

URSULA

That is the one thing I cannot do. No other man shall have me, if not you.

WILLIAM

I am not a man, Ursula. I am a cripple with a broken back—a stock, a stone—I am nothing. A marriage-bond with me would be a bond indeed. Let the dead past bury its dead. Our dream is over.

URSULA

" Sitting by the fire, seeing pictures in the fire, visions and dreams "—do you remember ?

WILLIAM

I have no dreams now—only nightmares. Nobody can bring back my dreams. Some of them even grudge me my work here—all that is left to me.

URSULA

I have broken what I cannot mend. William, tell me— had I at any time, even for a moment, any part in your dream ?

WILLIAM

I hardly know. But once, high in a corner of the clerestory, where none but God will look for it, I carved an angel with your face.

URSULA

Ah, my dear ! . . . And you will still have me go ?

WILLIAM

Yes; go. I am sorry. Go.

[URSULA *goes without protest.*

Father Theodatus ! (THEODATUS *looks in*) Pray conduct the Lady Ursula to the convent gate and ask the Father Prior if he can come and see me.

THEODATUS

I will, my son.

[*Exit* THEODATUS *with* URSULA, *right.*

CHOIR

My days are consumed away like smoke, and my bones are burnt up as it were a fire-brand.

My heart is smitten down and withered like grass, so that I forget to eat my bread.

For the voice of my groaning, my bones will scarce cleave to my flesh.

And that because of Thine indignation and wrath; for Thou hast taken me up and cast me down.

[*Enter* PRIOR, *right.*

PRIOR

You sent for me, my son ?

WILLIAM

Yes. I scarcely know why, save that I am in hell and can see no way out.

PRIOR

Is there some sin troubling your conscience?

WILLIAM

All the sins there are—or most of them, any way. Not that they ever troubled me till I was punished for them. But now—they rise up round me in the night and stifle me.

PRIOR

My son, will you not confess them and receive absolution?

WILLIAM

Confess? if I were to confess them all, you would be here till to-morrow. I cannot remember when I last made a confession.

PRIOR (*removing the papers from the stool up-stage and sitting down*)

In general, then, my son, and as well as you can remember them, tell me your sins.

WILLIAM

I do confess to God
The Father and the Son and Holy Ghost,
To Mary Mother of God the ever-virgin,
To the most holy Apostles Peter and Paul,
To blessed Michael and all his angels
And the whole company of Heaven, and thee,
Father, that I have sinned exceedingly,
In thought, in word, in action, by my fault,
By my own fault, my own most grievous fault.
I have lusted as men lust; I have eaten and drunk
With the drunken; I have given way to wrath,

Taking God's name in vain, cursing and smiting;
I have been too much eager after gold
And the brave things of the world, that take the eye
And charm the flesh. Now, smitten in my flesh
My sins have left me, and I see perforce
How worthless they all were. I am sorry for them.
Though yet I think I was not the worse craftsman
Because in me the lusty flesh rejoiced,
Lending its joy to all I did. Some men,
Fettering the body, fetter the soul, too,
So that the iron eats inward; thereof come
Cruelties, deceits, perversities of malice,
Strange twistings of the mind, defeats of spirit,
Whereof I cannot with sincerity
Accuse myself. But if it be a sin
To make the flesh the pander to the mind,
I have sinned deep. Of the means, not of the end,
I heartily repent.

PRIOR

Son, they mistake

Who think God hates those bodies which He made
Freedom, not licence, must be given the body,
For licence preys upon itself and others,
Devouring freedom's gifts. Have others suffered
Through lust, wrath, greed of yours?

WILLIAM

I do confess it,
And ask their pardon and God's pardon for it
Most humbly.

115

PRIOR

In this world as in God's heaven
There is no power to match humility:
It breaks the horns of the unicorns, and makes
The wand of justice flower like Aaron's rod.
Stoop to repent, and God will stoop to pardon.

WILLIAM

I do repent.

PRIOR

Indeed I hope thou dost.
For all these injuries, see thou make amends
So far as may be done; the irreparable
God's grace shall turn to good, since only He
Can lead out triumph from the gates of hell,
As He hath done by thee, using thy faults
To further His great ends, by His sole power,
Not Thine.

WILLIAM

I understand. A year ago
An idle mason let the chisel slip
Spoiling the saint he carved. I chid him for it,
Then took the tool and in that careless stroke
Saw a new vision, and so wrought it out
Into a hippogriff. But yet the mason
Was not the less to blame. So works with us
The cunning craftsman, God.

PRIOR

Thou hast a mind
Apt to receive His meaning. But take heed:

The mind hath its own snares. What sins of the mind
Trouble thee now?

WILLIAM

I do not know of any.

PRIOR

I cannot read the heart; but I am old
And know how little one need fear the flesh
In comparison of the mind. Think, I beseech thee,
If any sin lie yet upon thy conscience.

WILLIAM

Father, I know of none.

PRIOR

The Tree of Life
Grew by the Tree of Knowledge; and when Adam
Ate of the one, this doom was laid upon him
Never, but by self-knowledge, to taste life.
Pray now for grace, that thou may'st know and live.

WILLIAM

Wilt thou not give me present absolution?

PRIOR

Of all thy fleshly faults, humbly confessed,
Truly repented, I do absolve thee now
In the name of the Father and of the Son and of
The Holy Ghost. Amen.

GH

WILLIAM

Amen.

PRIOR

Good night;

Peace be with thee.

WILLIAM

And with thy spirit. Good night.

[*Exit* PRIOR. WILLIAM *tosses restlessly.*

℣. The ministers of God are sons of thunder, they are
falls of water, trampling of horses, and running of
chariots; and if the voices of these ministers cannot
overcome thy music, thy security, yet the Angels'
trumpets will.

[*Distant trumpet.*

CHOIR

Quantus tremor est futurus
Quando judex est venturus
Cuncta stricte discussurus.

[GABRIEL *goes up and stands behind* WILLIAM.

Tuba mirum spargens sonum
Per sepulchra regionum
Coget omnes ante thronum.

[MICHAEL *goes up and stands with drawn sword before*
WILLIAM.

Liber scriptus proferetur
In quo totum continetur
Unde mundus judicetur

[CASSIEL *goes up and stands at the foot of* WILLIAM's *bed,*
with the Book open before him.

Quid sum miser tunc dicturus,
Quem patronem rogaturus,
Cum vix justus sit securus ?

[RAPHAEL *goes up and stands with his censer at the head of*
WILLIAM'S *bed.*

WILLIAM

Sleep ! while these voices wail through aisle and cloister
Howling on judgment ? Cannot Father Ambrose
Keep his monks quiet—let a sick man rest ?
I am confessed, absolved. Why think of judgment ?
My soul is heavy even unto death,
And something not myself moves in the dusk
Fearfully. Lights ! lights ! lights !

GABRIEL (*laying his hand on* WILLIAM'S *eyes*)
Let there be light !

[WILLIAM *becomes aware of the presence of the* ANGELS.

℣. Behold, the angel of the Lord, standing in the way, and
his sword drawn in his hand.

℞. And he was afraid, because of the sword of the angel
of the Lord.

℣. My flesh trembleth for fear of Thee, and I am afraid of
Thy judgments.

℞. God is a righteous judge, strong and patient, and God
is provoked every day.

WILLIAM

So—it is come; first death and then the judgment.
Thou standest there and holdest up the Book
Wherein my sins show black. But I am shriven.

Christ's blood hath washed me white. What then art thou,
Threats in thy hand, and in thy face a threat
Sterner than steel and colder?

MICHAEL

I am Michael,
The sword of God. The edge is turned toward thee:
Not for those sins whereof thou dost repent,
Lust, greed, wrath, avarice, the faults of flesh
Sloughed off with the flesh, but that which feeds the soul,
The sin that is so much a part of thee
Thou know'st it not for sin.

WILLIAM

What sin is that?
Angel, what sins remain? I have envied no man,
Sought to rob no man of renown or merits,
Yea, praised all better workmen than myself
From an ungrudging heart. I have not been slothful—
Thou canst not say I was. Lust, greed, wrath, avarice,
None ever came between my work and me;
That I put first; never by nights of lust
Too spent to labour in the dawning day;
Never so drunken that I could not set
Level to stone or hold the plumb-line true;
Never so wroth as to confound my judgment
Between the man and the work, or call the one
Ill-done because I wished the other ill;
Never so grasping as to take reward
For what I did not, or despised to do.

If I neglected lip-service to God,
My hands served for me, and I wrought His praise
Not in light words puffed from a slumberous mind
Like wind, but in enduring monuments,
Symbol and fruit of that which works, not sleeps.
Answer me, Angel, what have I ever done
Or left undone, that I may not repent
Nor God forgive?

MICHAEL

        There where thy treasure is
Thy heart is also. Sin is of the heart.

WILLIAM

But all my heart was in my work.

MICHAEL

               Even so.

WILLIAM

What, in my work? The sin was in my work?
Thou liest. Though thou speak with God's own voice
Thou liest. In my work? That cannot be.
I grant the work not perfect; no man's work
Is perfect; but what hand and brain could do,
Such as God made them, that I did. Doth God
Demand the impossible? Then blame God, not me,
That I am man, not God. He hath broken me,
Hath sought to snatch the work out of my hand——
Wherefore? . . . O now, now I begin to see.
This was well said, He is a jealous God;
The work was not ill done—'twas done too well;
He will not have men creep so near His throne

To steal applause from Him. Is *this* my fault?
Why, this needs no repentance, and shall have none.
Let Him destroy me, since He has the power
To slay the thing He envies—but while I have breath
My work is mine; He shall not take it from me.

MICHAEL

No; thou shalt lay it down of thine own will.

WILLIAM

Never. Let Him heap on more torments yet——

MICHAEL

He can heap none on thee, He hath not borne——

WILLIAM

Let Him strike helpless hands as well as feet——

MICHAEL

Whose Feet and Hands were helpless stricken through——

WILLIAM

Scourge me and smite me and make blind mine eyes——

MICHAEL

As He was blindfolded and scourged and smitten——

WILLIAM

Dry up my voice in my throat and make me dumb——

MICHAEL

As He was dumb and opened not His mouth——

WILLIAM

Cramp me with pains——·

MICHAEL

As He was cramped with pains,
Racked limb from limb upon the stubborn Cross——

WILLIAM

Parch me with fever——

MICHAEL

He that cried, " I thirst "——

WILLIAM

Wring out my blood and sweat——

MICHAEL

Whose sweat, like blood,
Watered the garden in Gethsemane——

WILLIAM

For all that He can do I will not yield,
Nor leave to other men that which is mine,
To botch—to alter—turn to something else,
Not mine.

MICHAEL

Thou wilt not ? Yet God bore this too,
The last, the bitterest, worst humiliation,
Bowing His neck under the galling yoke
Frustrate, defeated, half His life unlived,
Nothing achieved.

WILLIAM

Could God, being God, do this ?

Christ, being man, did this; but still, through faith
Knew what He did. As gold and diamond,
Weighed in the chemist's balance, are but earth
Like tin or iron, albeit within them still
The purchase of the world lie implicit:
So, when God came to test of mortal time
In nature of a man whom time supplants,
He made no reservation of Himself
Nor of the godlike stamp that franked His gold,
But in good time let time supplant Him too.
The earth was rent, the sun's face turned to blood,
But He, unshaken, with exultant voice
Cried, " It is finished ! " and gave up the ghost.
" Finished "—when men had thought it scarce begun.
Then His disciples with blind faces mourned,
Weeping: " We trusted that He should redeem
Israel; but now we know not." What said He
Behind the shut doors in Jerusalem,
At Emmaus, and in the bitter dawn
By Galilee ? " I go; but feed My sheep;
For Me the Sabbath at the long week's close—
For you the task, for you the tongues of fire."
Thus shalt thou know the Master Architect,
Who plans so well, He may depart and leave
The work to others. Art thou more than God ?
Not God Himself was indispensable,
For lo ! God died—and still His work goes on.

℣. Thou that destroyest the temple and buildest it in three

days, save thyself. If thou be the Son of God, come down from the cross.

R℣. Thinkest thou that I cannot now pray to My Father, and He shall presently give Me more than twelve legions of angels ? But how then shall the scriptures be fulfilled, that thus it must be ?

RAPHAEL

Lord, I believe; help Thou mine unbelief.

WILLIAM

Lord, I believe; help Thou mine unbelief.

CHOIR

Faithful Cross, above all other
One and only noble Tree,
None in foliage, none in blossom,
None in fruit thy peer may be;
Sweetest wood and sweetest iron,
Sweetest weight is hung on thee.

WILLIAM

O, I have sinned. The eldest sin of all,
Pride, that struck down the morning star from Heaven
Hath struck down me from where I sat and shone
Smiling on my new world. All other sins
God will forgive but that. I am damned, damned,
Justly. Yet, O most just and merciful God,
Hear me but once, Thou that didst make the world
And wilt not let one thing that Thou hast made,
No, not one sparrow, perish without Thy Will

125

(Since what we make, we love)—for that love's sake
Smite only me and spare my handiwork.
Jesu, the carpenter's Son, the Master-builder,
Architect, poet, maker—by those hands
That Thine own nails have wounded—by the wood
Whence Thou didst carve Thy Cross—let not the Church
Be lost through me. Let me lie deep in hell,
Death gnaw upon me, purge my bones with fire,
But let my work, all that was good in me,
All that was God, stand up and live and grow.
The work is sound, Lord God, no rottenness there—
Only in me. Wipe out my name from men
But not my work; to other men the glory
And to Thy Name alone. But if to the damned
Be any mercy at all, O send Thy spirit
To blow apart the sundering flames, that I
After a thousand years of hell, may catch
One glimpse, one only, of the Church of Christ,
The perfect work, finished, though not by me.

℣. Save me from the lion's mouth; Thou hast heard me
also from among the horns of the unicorns.

℞. For why ? Thou shalt not leave my soul in hell, neither
shalt Thou suffer Thine holy one to see corruption.

[*Trumpet.*

CASSIEL

Sheathe thy sword, Michael; the fight is won.

RAPHAEL

Close the book, Cassiel; the score is paid.

GABRIEL

Give glory, Raphael; the race is run.

MICHAEL

Lead homeward, Gabriel, the sheep that strayed.

ALL

Eloi, Eloi, Eloi,
Glory to God in the highest; holy is He !

MICHAEL

How hardly shall the rich man enter in
To the Kingdom of Heaven ! By what sharp, thorny ways,
By what strait gate at last ! But when he is come,
The angelic trumpets split their golden throats
Triumphant, to the stars singing together
And all the sons of God shouting for joy.
Be comforted, thou that wast rich in gifts;
For thou art broken on the self-same rack
That broke the richest Prince of all the world,
The Master-man. Thou shalt not surely die,
Save as He died; nor suffer, save with Him;
Nor lie in hell, for He hath conquered hell
And flung the gates wide open. They that bear
The cross with Him, with Him shall wear a crown
Such as the angels know not. Then be still,
And know that He is God, and God alone.

℣. Who suffered for our salvation; descended into hell,
rose again the third day from the dead.

℟. He ascended into Heaven, He sitteth on the right hand
of the Father, God Almighty; from whence He shall
come to judge the quick and the dead.

CHOIR

Eloi, Eloi, Eloi,

Glory to God in the highest; holy is He !

[*While this is sung, the* ANGELS *go up and stand side by side across the stage behind the couch.*

WILLIAM

I shall not die but live, and declare the works of the
Lord. Who is there ? I was dreaming. Gervase ! Hubert !

[GERVASE *and* HUBERT *run in, left and right.*

GERVASE

William ?

HUBERT

Dear master ?

WILLIAM

God hath changed my mind.
I must submit. I must go back to France.
I do but hinder the work, lingering here,
Kicking against the pricks.

GERVASE

Do not say so !

HUBERT

What should we do without you ?

WILLIAM

I am not
The only architect in the world—there are others
Will do the work as well, better perhaps.
Stay not to chide me—listen, there is one,
William the Englishman, a little man,

But with a mounting spirit and great vision;
Send now for him. I think we quarrelled once,
Not seeing eye to eye—but that is nothing;
He will respect my work as I do his,
And build a harmony of his and mine
To a nobler close than mine. I'll not dictate
Conditions to the Chapter; but, should they choose
William the Englishman to follow me,
He'll do such work for them as honours God
And them and all good craftsmen. As for me,
My place is here no more. I am in God's hand.
Take me and bear me hence.

HUBERT
                Dear master, whither?

WILLIAM
To the Lady Ursula's lodging. If unto her
I can make any amends, then I will make it.
To all of you, I owe a debt of love
Which I will pay with love. Only to God,
That royal creditor, no debt remains.
He from the treasure of His great heart hath paid
The whole sum due, and cancelled out the bond.

GERVASE
Laus Deo!

  [GERVASE *and* HUBERT *carry* WILLIAM *out, right.*

CHOIR
O quanta qualia sunt illa sabbata,
Quae semper celebrat superna curia,

Quae fessis requies, quae merces fortibus,
Cum erit omnia Deus in omnibus.

Vere Jerusalem illic est civitas,
Cujus pax jugis est summa jucunditas,
Ubi non praevenit rem desiderium,
Nec desiderio minus est praemium.

Illic ex sabbato succedit sabbatum,
Perpes laetitia sabbatizantium,
Nec ineffabiles cessabunt jubili,
Quos decantabimus et nos et angeli.

[MICHAEL *comes down to the foot of the steps and addresses the congregation; the other three* ANGELS *standing above him.*

MICHAEL

Children of men, lift up your hearts. Laud and magnify God, the everlasting Wisdom, the holy, undivided and adorable Trinity.

Praise Him that He hath made man in His own image, a maker and craftsman like Himself, a little mirror of His triune majesty.

For every work of creation is threefold, an earthly trinity to match the heavenly.

First: there is the Creative Idea; passionless, timeless, beholding the whole work complete at once, the end in the beginning; and this is the image of the Father.

Second: there is the Creative Energy, begotten of that Idea, working in time from the beginning to the end, with sweat and passion, being incarnate in the bonds of matter; and this is the image of the Word.

Third: there is the Creative Power, the meaning of the work and its response in the lively soul; and this is the image of the indwelling Spirit.

And these three are one, each equally in itself the whole work, whereof none can exist without other; and this is the image of the Trinity.

Look then upon this Cathedral Church of Christ: imagined by men's minds, built by the labour of men's hands, working with power upon the souls of men; symbol of the everlasting Trinity, the visible temple of God.

As you would honour Christ, so honour His Church; nor suffer this temple of His Body to know decay.

FINIS

THE DOROTHY L. SAYERS SOCIETY

THE DOROTHY L. SAYERS Society, with now some 500 members worldwide, was founded in her hometown of Witham in 1976. Its aims are educational: to collect and preserve archival material, to act as a centre of advice for scholars and researchers, and to present the name of Dorothy L. Sayers to the public by encouraging publication and performance of her works and by making grants and awards. We have close links with the Marion E. Wade Center at Wheaton College, Illinois, where the majority of her papers are held.

An annual Convention is held with at least half a dozen further meetings not only in UK, but we have also met in USA, Germany, Sweden, France and The Netherlands, studying themes ranging from Incunabula, fungal poisons and Dante, to Education and the Nicene Creed. We have held concerts of music, have sponsored performances of The Zeal of thy House in Canterbury Cathedral, the Bach B Minor Mass in Oxford, and new incidental music for our production of some of The Man Born to be King plays in London. 1993 saw the Centenary of the birth of Dorothy L. Sayers with over 30 events worldwide. Her poem "The Three Kings" was set as a carol, and performed and broadcast in the Midnight service at Canterbury Cathedral.

Our publications include the Poetry of Dorothy L. Sayers, five volumes of The Letters of Dorothy L. Sayers, and, most recently, two hitherto unpublished talks by DLS, Les origines du roman policier, and The Christ of the Creeds. We have extensive archives.

Witham now has a Dorothy L. Sayers Centre in the public library where we hold an annual Sayers Lecture and a statue of DLS with her cat Blitz.

Further information is available from the Society's headquarters at Rose Cottage, Malthouse Lane, Hurstpierpoint, West Sussex BN6 9JY or the web site: http://www.sayers.org.uk

Christopher Dean
DLS Society Chairman
2011

CPSIA information can be obtained
at www.ICGtesting.com
Printed in the USA
LVHW052314100122
708185LV00013B/1651